James Pickles wa[...] 1925, the son of [...] radio broadcaste[...] Worksop College, he read law at Leeds University and received an MA from Christ Church, Oxford. Married in 1948, he has two sons, and a daughter, the actress Carolyn Pickles.

He was called to the Bar in 1948, practising from chambers in Bradford. From 1963 he sat as an assistant recorder at quarter sessions, and was promoted to recorder of the Crown Court in 1972. Since 1976, he has been known principally for his work as a Circuit Judge sitting in the Crown and County Courts, mainly in Yorkshire, but also in London. He retired from the bench in 1991.

His previous books, *Straight From The Bench* and *Judge For Yourself* were both non-fiction bestsellers. He has written many articles for national newspapers and is regularly invited to give his controversial views on legal issues on TV and radio, and in after-dinner speeches. *Off the Record* is his first novel.

Also by James Pickles:

STRAIGHT FROM THE BENCH
JUDGE FOR YOURSELF

Off The
Record

JAMES PICKLES

WARNER BOOKS

A *Warner* Book

First published in Great Britain in 1993
by Smith Gryphon Limited
This edition published by Warner Books in 1995

Copyright © James Pickles 1993

The moral right of the author has been asserted.

A CIP catalogue for this book
is available from the British Library

ISBN 0 7515 1016 5

Prtinted and bound in Great Britain by
Clays Ltd, St. Ives, plc

Warner Books
A Division of
Little, Brown and Company (UK)
Brettenham House
Lancaster Place
London WC2E 7EN

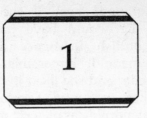

1

PRIVATE SECRETARY Mrs Anona 'No-Knickers' Chandelle-Sweet nodded to the policeman at the gate and casually showed her ID card to the man in security. Then she took the lift to the second-floor flat over her employer's office, unlocked the door, went straight to her boss's bedroom and entered without knocking. At 8.50 a.m. he was still in bed, naked and waiting for her.

There was barely a grunt of greeting from either of them as she took off her coat, then the rest of her clothes. Thirty-four years had barely started to deform Anona's nubile pneumatic body. A blue-eyed blonde with large luscious lips and ample proud tits, she was built for sex and practised it avidly. Only her gluttony for food – which promised some day to turn her curves into billows – might eventually threaten the daily slaking of her appetite. Her naked employer – his nickname was 'Trot' – lifted the bed-clothes aside for her entry and made ready for his.

Anona knew what was to come. Their routine took place most weekdays at this time, but she did not relish the first course of the sexual meal. In fact she detested the taste of Trot's prick, though she endured it as part of the package that guaranteed her this prestigious post. If she could have avoided it, she would have done, but her employer's bullish insistence and lack of imagination made it impossible. The second course was better and she liked it: the transfer of the action to her own centre of sensation.

And so, that morning as on most mornings, Trot clambered heavily on top. He was a bulky paunchy man of fifty-six, with thinning hair. No-one had ever called him good-looking, except to his florid face and large purple beacon nose, though he himself saw his body as handsome and rugged. He positioned himself missionarily, but Anona's missionary zeal was less than it had been when she started working for him – and under him – two-and-a-half years previously. This part of the action was better, for her, though. Compared with the preliminaries it was a different ball-game.

Balls-game? Never mind the words, feel the thrusts, she thought. The piston thrusts: they were better. She didn't get enough from her weak barrister husband, now a Circuit judge of all things; not even from her twenty year old toy-boy Dennis, so handsome and trusting. He said he loved her and he probably thought he did, but he found her so exciting he often came too soon. As for her boss, at least he went on longer. Nowadays even too long, as he was doing that moment, pressing on like a long-distance runner who had to reach the winning-post or retire forever, and wasn't fit enough but carried on doggedly, all the same.

If she had to choose on raw performance she would choose this man. Not a nice man, but stronger than toy-boy Dennis and bigger and firmer than flabby husband Alwyne. On the nowadays rare occasions that he did manage to inflate, Alwyne detumesced almost immediately, never rising to the ramming posture properly and sometimes falling asleep while vainly trying to negotiate her willing though unthrilled body.

She was fair to the male sex as a group, Anona mused, as Trot trotted on with growing desperation. She serviced the young, the middle-aged and the old – although her employer would prefer to be referred to as middle-aged too. You could leave out romance, with all three; she had abandoned it years ago. Men were not romantic, only randy. They thought with their pricks, were obsessed with them in fact. A man without his prick would be no man at all.

She couldn't imagine this man without his, for example. They were both hooked on sex and that is why they had been having it so often. She vividly recalled one memorable day when she had had it twice with Trot, once with toy-boy Dennis and again with husband Alwyne, all within twenty-four hours. Some day, that. Pleasure magnified as if by an electrical transformer that had left her shaking with slaked sensuality – and to be honest just a bit sore – for about twelve hours. She hadn't been so active since her three years at university in the United States.

3

Christened Anona Nickerton, she was unkindly though accurately nicknamed 'No-Knickers' at Heatherstones, an exclusive boarding school which prepared girls for the social rigours of life in the Home Counties, and the name had stuck. Her father, a Tory Cabinet Minister at the time, had sent her away to school at eleven to make a lady of her, but at fifteen she had made a man out of the biology teacher Mr Ethelred McNab, BA. Poor Ethelred's scientific studies had left him ill-equipped for practical biology of Anona's sort, and unprepared to repel the assaults of randy teenagers. He was twenty-four and a virgin. She was not, having at fourteen waylaid a newspaper boy who happened to call at her home while she was alone. The newspaper boy had expected to insert the *Daily Express* through the Nickertons' letter-box. Instead he found himself – or part of himself – being inserted at an express rate through another aperture.

Mr McNab succumbed with No-Knickers on top, as they lay under a table in the biology lab – an appropriate place in many ways. When they were confronted by the headmistress while *in flagrante delicto*, he was asked what he thought he was doing but found it difficult to think up a plausible tale and so was dismissed instantly.

In practical terms he had learnt more from his ardent pupil than she from him, and he soon married and forsook teaching for sex-counselling. Anona, who was not expelled – the spinster headmistress assumed she was an innocent victim of McNab's lust – thought she had done him a good turn. But she also thought the headmistress had been a little unfair in allotting all the blame to the susceptible biology master.

Anona was even more popular with the males at the American university where she went on to study modern literature – that being the only vacancy the young dean could make for her when she went for interview, breasts first. He had never goggled at such a pair, could not take his eyes off them or wait to get his hands on them, which he did within twenty-four hours.

After that there was no holding her. Or rather she was held by practically all of the male students except the gays (about one in five). For three years she performed nightly or even twice-nightly, going through the campus like a molten meteorite through ice.

No-Knickers stole a glance at her watch, carefully concealing the gesture. Her employer might think she was bored, as indeed she was starting to be. The piston job was okay, but at this rate she'd soon need a re-bore. Maybe she was in the wrong job. There were disadvantages to her position with this ageing ramrod, who was slackening speed and at any moment might opt out of the race.

By now the fat man was feeling like a fat old man. His spirit was strong but his flesh was flabby and he knew he could not win this one. These bouts were held most mornings after he had spent the night in the flat, while his lady wife Lady Emeline was safely stowed away at their country seat in Little Thatching, Sussex. There she chased foxes unsuccessfully, harried people lower than her in the social register successfully, and ran the local Conservative Women's Group, the Society for Distressed Gentlefolk and the Loyal Society of St George indifferently.

He stopped and rolled off.

'Sorry, Nonie. Can't manage it today.'

'No need to apologise,' she murmured, as relieved as the bed-springs were and a good deal quieter than they had been.

Trot got out of bed, went to the door of the flat and collected a clutch of newspapers that had been fed through the letter-box. He looked at the *Courier* first.

'That fucker,' he mouthed as he saw the splash story on the front. 'That fucker's been at it again.'

'What is it now, Trot?' Her employer's full name was Lord Oswald Trentham Trotter of St Pancras, Lord High Chancellor of Great Britain and Northern Ireland, holder of the Great Seal. He now stood before her pulling up his underpants and preparing for the more official rigours of the day. Soon he would be donning the eighteenth-century morning-coat, knee-breeches, black silk stockings, buckled shoes, ruffle and full-bottom wig he wore for presiding over the Upper House of Parliament.

The newspaper that he was reading reported a speech made by Mr Justice Raymond Slingsby the previous evening to magistrates at Barfield on the North Midland Circuit. The speech criticised the system whereby the Lord Chancellor alone appointed judges. The system was wide open to nepotism or worse, the judge had said, and Trot was appalled to read his suggestion that all was not well concerning the recent appointment as a circuit judge of Alwyne Chandelle-Sweet, the husband of the Lord Chancellor's private secretary. Mr Justice Slingsby said he knew the man well, and he did not consider him a suitable candidate for the bench.

Trot saw with horror the words, 'One can only assume that the relationship between the Lord Chancellor and his private secretary must be more than has so far appeared and more than her duties strictly require.'

He was too shocked to speak. His position was under attack again by that appalling socialist judge from the north. Slingsby would have to be dealt with. The Lord Chancellor intended to assert himself.

Lord Trotter had won some glittering prizes. Some of them, though, glistered but were not gold. After Westminster School – where he went because Eton did not rate young Trot's academic level as highly as he and his father did – he coasted to Christ Church, Oxford. The bridge between the two academic establishments was still strong enough after centuries of traffic to bear the weight of dim young Trot.

At university he chose medieval history on the correct assumption that there would be few student rivals in that discipline, but the incorrect assumption that he was therefore likely to win first-class honours and become a professor. He scraped a third, which was generous.

His father, Sir Julian Trotter, Bart., had been sent down from the same college for idleness. He had had to go into the City, which was the only more-or-less respectable lucrative occupation that would accept him. He put his son into the law for the same reason. Oswald Trotter was welcomed into fashionable civil chambers in the Temple by the head, who had been at Eton with his father, and rose effortlessly by specialising in libel and slander – a useful field for one intending to enter the bent world of politics.

In the 1964 general election, at the age of twenty-eight, Trot stood for the safe Tory seat of Addingup in Surrey, then in the Rolex and Roller stockbroker belt, later to become the Jaguar and Jail locale. He was financed by his father, then the head of a go-go (soon to be gone-gone) syndicate at Lloyds of London.

Sadly for Trot, his father disappeared from public life almost immediately afterwards, owing to a little matter of company fraud, which saw him descending the steps leading from the dock of the Old Bailey's No. 1 court to Dartmoor.

His son would have been there to raise a farewell finger or two had he not been engaged in No. 2 court defending a forger – one who had the impudence to suggest he should pay his lawyers in new £20 notes. Trot himself said he would take the risk if his fee was doubled, but his instructing solicitors, an old conservative firm, had advised against it. They said it would be unprofessional and indeed unsafe, knowing more about the defendant's past than they thought it prudent to commit to counsel's brief.

Year by year Trot rose steadily towards the top of the Tory party, by having a capable secretary to say and do the right things in answer to constituents' letters, and by relying on that centuries-old English principle of political preferment – Buggins's Turn. At forty he became a QC. He took silk, or rather had it thrust upon him by Lord Chancellor Bagworthy of Blackpool who had been a close friend of his father's and had defended him at the Bailey.

Baggers had made a balls of it by not being present in court for most of the trial, as he had several important cases going on in London concurrently. When he did arrive for Sir Julian Trotter's fraud case, he muddled up the brief with one of dangerous driving, so that his final speech – his only contribution to the proceedings – baffled the judge, entertained the jury and gratified the Serious Fraud Office, who were delighted to register a conviction after a long run of acquittals. After that, the least Baggers could do was give his old friend's son the leg-up he was sure he deserved.

'Which fucker? What's he been doing?' No-Knickers, still in bed, repeated her question.

'That bloody man Slingsby,' Lord Trotter said as he tried for the fourth time to adjust his ruffle. 'He's criticised me again – about the people I've made judges.'

'Didn't *you* appoint *him*?'

'It was that confounded Labour Lord

Chancellor Henry Wetherington. Worst one this century.'

'I bet you run him close, Trot.'

No-Knickers' attempt to lighten the air went unacknowledged. She knew she'd gone too far, and that Trot could be storing up one of his rages. But he had Slingsby on his mind and he wouldn't retaliate till later.

Apprehensively, Trot selected the *Sun*. Its splash was JUDGE FLAYS HIS BOSS. In smaller type: Nepotism alleged. Nonie would have to know, he thought, showing her the paper.

She burst out of bed, her ample form shaking and bouncing. 'They're talking about *me*? No!' Together they read the *Sun*'s report.

'The fucker. The nerve of the man. The bloody nerve. He's gone too far this time!'

'Is he saying that . . . that you gave the job to Alwyne because . . .' Anona stuttered.

'Because of you and me.'

'But didn't you?'

'Don't be ridiculous, Nonie.'

Anona stared at him in surprise. 'But when Alwyne started getting suspicious, I thought you said there was only one way of shutting him up.'

'You've got it wrong,' snarled Trot. 'I always go for merit. And for that bewigged bastard Slingsby to attack me, in public, to magistrates of all people. I *appointed* a lot of them myself. In my name anyway.'

'What's going to happen then, Trot?'

'I shall get him.'

Anona was having difficulty encasing her

bulging breasts in her bra, but Trot wasn't going to help her – he had problems of his own, and the ruffle wasn't the only one.

'How *can* you get Slingsby?' she persisted.

'I shall have him sacked!'

'But how, Trot?'

'An address by both Houses of Parliament to the Queen.'

'Has it ever happened?'

'Never heard of it, but there'll be a way. If he doesn't shut up, there has to be a way. He must be destroyed before he destroys . . .'

'Us?' squeaked Anona.

'We mustn't think of ourselves, Nonie. It's the judiciary that matters. Public confidence. That bastard Slingsby with his socialist nonsense. Treachery, that's what it is, treachery. He should be put in the Tower.'

'Isn't that a bit OTT, OTT?'

'No need to be clever,' snapped Trot. He was beginning to dislike her. But those breasts, as she struggled to fasten her bra; those oozing, bubbling, nuzzlable breasts. They were almost past their best but he would never be past the breast – he was a breasts-man, always had been and always would be. It wouldn't be easy to abandon those kneadable kissable fondlable appendages. It was so convenient to have them always on tap.

There was also an even stronger reason for retaining Nonie's services: she knew too much. There were only two ways of getting rid – paying her off or knocking her off, and he shrank from

11

both. The first was too costly and the second too risky.

The Lord Chancellor did not know, and it would have enraged him to find out, that after his predecessor, the hated socialist Lord Wetherington of Welshpool, had lost office he had had to pay Nonie £25,000 for concealing their high jinks in that very same bedroom. Trot would have strangled her had he known, but like all good private secretaries, Anona Chandelle-Sweet was discreet. She thought of herself as politically even-handed, as a civil servant should be. A man's politics were far less important than his prick. She never discussed her own political views at work, though she told her friends she was a Progressive Fascist, because it shocked them mildly to hear it.

In reality she had no time or inclination for politics. She was happy to serve any Lord Chancellor who happened to lounge on the Woolsack. 'Wet' Wetherington had been a disappointment to almost everyone, however. His performances when addressing the Upper House had been as pathetic as his performances in the upper position when fucking his private secretary.

His sexual and political antics were equally kinky, Anona had felt. What true socialist would dress up like Dame Edna in drag for Parliament, then minutes later don his bra, pants and suspenders for sex with her? But duty was duty, and fucking was fucking, and No-Knickers, who had expensive tastes, was prepared to combine the two, provided there was a financial pay-off in view.

'Slingsby has to be destroyed, and quickly, before he destroys the lot of us – the whole system, the centuries old system, hallowed by time,' the Lord Chancellor insisted pompously.

'Are you going to have his throat cut then, Trot?' asked Anona in an innocent voice.

'Absurd.'

'Have you had to get rid of other High Court judges?'

'There's been nobody like Slingsby, ever, thank God. But there'll be something in his life we can get him for. Everybody has something.'

'Even you, Trot?'

The Lord Chancellor ignored her question. 'There are some letters to be typed. I suggest you do them; I have to go and see Kingston.' Determined to assert himself, the holder of the Great Seal set off in search of his permanent secretary, Sir Anthony Kingston KCB.

One hundred and fifty miles north, at Barfield, the Honourable Mr Justice Raymond Slingsby was examining the *Courier* as he lingered over a late breakfast with his wife Helen. The judge – tall, slim, balding but still handsome – was not due to sit at the Crown Court till 11 o'clock that day. This was for the convenience of a barrister who had an urgent dental appointment to have a wisdom tooth out.

It was a pity, Raymond had thought, because the only wisdom Eric Wickstead-Hacking had was in his teeth. What a good idea it would be to have his voice removed too, since every time he used it he added another six months to his client's sentence.

Mr Justice Slingsby was on the North Midland Circuit – one of the six circuits in England and Wales – and he had been born and bred there too. Barfield, his home, was a northern industrial city that had seen more distinguished days. When Britain was the workshop of the world it was the wealthiest town in the world per head of population. Now the country had become the toyshop of the world, but the judges still came on circuit to Barfield and stayed at the same palatial 'Lodgings'. The only discernible difference was that the Rolls-Royce of old had been replaced by a more modest Mercedes.

Ray Slingsby was the son of a coal-miner who was both a Methodist and a socialist, as many working people had been fifty years ago. But now there were few Methodists, fewer socialists and virtually no-one who was both. Ray went to Barfield grammar school, and then the city's university, so most of his life had been lived there. If ever he took a peerage he would take the title Barfield – but heaven forbid he should betray his principles in that way. He was the only High Court judge in seven hundred years ever to refuse to be knighted. Normally a knighthood went with the job, and this heresy was so shocking that there was a leader in *The Times* condemning his attempt to sabotage the established order, and questions were asked in the House of Commons.

When, if ever, everybody had a bar-code that could be fed into a giant computer, Slingsby felt that his would identify him as a Barfield man through and through. He even supported Barfield Town at football and occasionally stood on the almost empty terraces watching a team that had always bounced along the bottom of the lowest division and whose players had to rely on the other side's own goals even to register a point.

The intensity of Ray's fight against the Lord Chancellor was something he found it hard to explain, even to himself. Why was he doing it and what did he hope to gain? He knew it was a question he would not be alone in asking as the final clash with Trotter approached.

The truth of it was, he did not know the answer. He was as he was and could not change himself. If he thought injustice was being done, he had to say so and try to put things right.

Perhaps it had something to do with his parents. His mother was a former weaver, a tough and outspoken woman who always said exactly what she thought. So did his father, a dedicated trade unionist, who stood up to the bosses. Raymond assumed that their example had rubbed off on him from his early years. He could give no other explanation for an anti-authority streak that went as far back as he could remember.

When he was only five he refused for days to go to school. He lost that first battle against authority, but he won all the others he could recollect. Most memorable was the strike he organised at school when Bob Ranson was caned for kissing a girl behind the bike-sheds. Ray went to the headmaster and told him it was hypocritical and wrong to punish Bob in that way, or indeed at all. He took his case to the Parent Teachers Association, and eventually the school dropped caning altogether. Ray learned then that you could beat the Establishment if your cause was just and you fought hard enough and with insight and intelligence.

The judge passed the *Courier* to his wife without a word as Mary, the large waitress who worked at the Lodgings, which were thoughtfully provided by the Lord Chancellor's Department for High Court judges visiting the city, squeezed by. Although the Slingsbys still had a house in Barfield, Ray was expected to stay at the Lodgings when sitting locally. He resented that but even his independence had its limits.

He did not like all the protocol involved in staying in Lodgings, such as dressing for dinner if the senior judge present decided upon it. There was no popping out to the pub. As for nipping round to the Working Men's Club where he had spent many hours while a Labour member of Barfield council and chairman of its Finance Committee – such a visit would be enough to have him reported to the Lord Chancellor, the appalling Trot who represented everything that was wrong with the law.

Trot, thought Ray, had the Achilles heel of his class, and as that was the upper-class, the Achilles heel of the whole nation. He thought he was always right. In fact, although he appointed all judges, he was the least judicial person in the realm. A good judge is fair and Trot was not;

listens to both sides and Trot was incapable of it; takes heed of criticism, but Trot dismissed it all with a wheezy chuckle. If in a hundred years' time people asked 'why did Britain go wrong?', the answer should be that it was because men like Lord Trotter self-confidently led the country down the drain, mouthing that Britain was the best country in the world and (the greatest fallacy of all) 'British justice is the best in the world.'

Ray looked across the table at his wife. Had he ever really got to know her in the twenty-four years they had been married? Her still uncreased face was bespectacled, her hair was grey and her shoulders were rounded with age, but she was still a very nice woman.

What a very pleasant woman, Slingsby thought to himself. How kind she was to children and animals; how charming with everybody. She had a word for all and the lower in the social scale they were, the kinder and longer the conversation. That was what had appealed to him when he was introduced to her at a church fete, soon after her father came to Barfield. He was a vicar then, but on his way to becoming bishop of Garbridge – inevitably corrupted to Garbage, though to be fair he was one of the better, less pompous bishops.

His daughter, Helen, had been to a posh boarding school and spoke with a deep upper-class voice, but she attracted Ray from the start because she had a loveliness, a serenity, that appealed to him. She never lost her temper or scolded people, which was a welcome contrast to his own home life where his miner father, though basically a good man, did lose his temper and swear a lot.

The problem was that Raymond had been so overwhelmed by the appearance of the goods – Helen – that he had omitted to test them fully before he acquired them on a lifetime contract. Helen had every virtue except that, to Ray, vital one – an interest in sex. She submitted to him dutifully at first and produced their daughter Anne, now nineteen and at Cardiff university studying English, but her obvious lack of enthusiasm had cooled Ray's ardour years ago.

Helen read the report on the front page of the *Courier*, then placed the paper carefully on the floor without opening it. She didn't want such papers in the house, with their nudes, and if this had been her house and not owned by the Lord Chancellor's Department, she would have forbidden it, as she had at home. As for so-called Page Three photographs, they *did* demean women and MP Clare Short, left-wing though she was, was right about that, she thought.

Ray's mind went off on another tangent. His parents were Edwardians with Victorian attitudes. They believed in Jesus, the Virgin Birth, the ascent of Jesus into Heaven like a kite, and an after-life. All myths. They believed you didn't have sex before marriage and that marriage lasted until death. He accepted it all until in his teens he met the real world, and his religious notions died a slow death.

What sexual frustration Ray felt he had endured over the years! He could not restrain his cantering mind as he munched his toast. What guilt when he had been tempted to stray, and what disaster on the one occasion he tried: the German teacher on the town-twinning trip to Rotenburg-Ober-Tauber eight years ago.

He had been weak in the first place to allow himself to be persuaded to join the group of prominent Barfield citizens visiting the German town. He didn't really approve of such expeditions, regarding them as a misuse of council funds, but the idea of a few days in Germany – on his own, because Helen had been involved with one of her many charity do's – had seemed very attractive at the time. He had to admit that the Germans had done them proud and that the whole expedition had been very enjoyable. Or at least it would have been, had it not been for the fiasco with the girl.

Hildegard Schlegel was on the Rotenburg-Ober-Tauber welcoming committee. She was an attractive fair girl with an earnest manner, who taught English in one of the local secondary schools. Slingsby, whose German was by no means fluent, was very pleased to find her sitting next to him at the welcoming dinner, and as the evening wore on he began to wonder if the keen interest Hildegard expressed in the English legal system reflected a degree of interest in himself as a man. It was an intoxicating thought, and though he tried to tell himself he was being a fool, he could not help being excited when he was placed next to her again at lunch the following day.

'I asked for you specially,' Hildegard told him,

'because so good a talk we had last night.' Slingsby glowed, and he was glowing still more when, after a substantial lunch and many bottles of local wine, the whole party set off on a coach trip to Schloss Grosserstein, a local tourist attraction. Hildegard sat beside him, chattering happily, and he could feel the warmth of her bare arm through his shirt. He was sure that she was leaning against him just a little bit and his pulses began to race.

The Schloss was ancient and turreted, standing high on a hill surrounded by forests. Inside, there were dimly lit corridors and flights of twisting steps leading to dark, echoing rooms full of huge carved pieces of furniture. The group was given a guided tour, but Slingsby and Hildegard found themselves lagging behind as Hildegard, who had obviously brought many school parties round the Schloss, added her own commentary to the guide's. Slingsby had drunk more than usual at lunch and his head was spinning a little. He was beginning to feel he needed to sit down.

Suddenly Hildegard grasped his hand and pulled him towards a flight of stairs. 'Come, this way. There is a most fantastic view.' They came out into a round turret room and Hildegard, still with his hand in hers, dragged him to the tall window set deep in the wall. 'Look, is it not beautiful?'

The view of hills and forest was spectacular, but Slingsby found himself overwhelmed by the nearness of Hildegard herself, squashed beside him in the narrow aperture. Unable to resist, he planted a clumsy kiss on her cheek and then, as she swung round towards him, tried to find her lips. She had her back to the window now and he put his arms around her, blocking her in to the recess. He was sure she was responding and his excitement grew, then all at once he realised that she was struggling to push him from her.

'Herr Slingsby, please.' Her voice in his ears sounded shrill and panic-stricken. He could not bear to let her go, but she twisted away and began to scream out of the window for help. Shocked, he backed away, realising that he had made a dreadful mistake. As he moved, Hildegard pushed past him, bright scarlet in the face, and fled from the room. He heard her echoing footsteps disappear down the stairs and followed slowly, feeling suddenly completely sober and very worried. Then followed a horrible half-hour of wandering round the castle, trying to find the rest of his party and dreading the reception he would get when he did.

In the event, it appeared that nobody had heard Hildegard's screams and that she had not told anyone else what had happened. When Slingsby appeared she gave him one furious glance and then ignored him completely for the remainder of the time the English and German parties spent together. He wanted to apologise, but he didn't think it would do any good. He knew he had misread her signals and been too hasty, and now she clearly didn't want him anywhere near her.

The whole episode put Slingsby off even looking at another woman for a long time. He had never strayed from that day to this and now, at fifty-one, he supposed that he never would. It was hopeless, he thought. He had lost out on the Permissive Society, been black-balled when he had applied to join it; frozen out. There were compensations, he supposed. At least he had a stable family life even though it was a sterile one.

Helen punctured his ballooning thoughts. 'It's too dangerous. I did warn you, Ray.'

'That speech to the magistrates?' He knew exactly what she was talking about, but he asked the question anyway.

'I know you like to say what you think, Ray, and I admire you for it. But where will it end? What will it get you, except publicity and controversy and more trouble with the Lord Chancellor? Is it worth it?'

'I shan't give in,' said Ray, stabbing his knife into the butter.

Helen sighed. She'd heard and seen it all before.

'Trotter is evil,' he went on, thrusting a spoon firmly into the marmalade pot. 'He has to be brought down.'

'He must think the same about you, Ray, and he's bigger than you. He has the power.'

'I couldn't let it go and leave things unfinished. I'd never live with it, Helen.' Ray bit off a large mouthful of toast and crunched it vigorously.

'I hope you don't die from it, dear,' said Helen.

Ray's expression was determined. 'I'll survive. I always have. I shall carry on my campaign till Trotter goes and the rotten system for appointing judges is reformed.'

'So it's war to the death.' She sighed again. This time the sigh took a little longer and was a little deeper. She knew Ray didn't give in, ever, when embattled with 'them', and especially not when the battle was with Lord Chancellor Trotter.

Helen admired her husband, with reservations. He did have principles and he was stuck to them with super-glue. But his principles caused trouble, controversy, press people besieging the house and flashing cameras as one tried to leave, however discreetly one did it. There were front-page headlines and photographs; sympathetic but irritating remarks by her middle-class friends, the ones Ray called 'socially incestuous'.

Ray was too busy and too indifferent to get involved in Helen's social life of coffee-mornings, RSPCA lunches and church fetes, and even Helen was not a firm believer if she went deeply into it – something that on the whole she didn't find necessary. But the church and other charity groups had nice people in them, people from her class. Even though Helen would never put it that way, regarding herself as classless – which Ray said no-one could be in class-dominated Britain.

She reverted to the practical. 'This reference to the Lord Chancellor and his private secretary. You hinted there was something wrong going on.'

'There is. I'm certain,' said Ray.

'But you of all people should know you need evidence.'

'There's no other explanation for him putting her husband on the Circuit bench.' Ray's indignation grew as he went on, 'I know Alwyne

Chandelle-Sweet, as he calls himself. He's a nonentity. He's a few years junior to me. He wasn't in my chambers but I saw him do cases. He's done some before me – pleas of guilty mostly. He never had much of a practice. No brain; there's nothing to him. He'll be an appalling judge. I don't think he's even sat as an assistant recorder – and that's the lowest form of judicial life.'

Helen tried again. 'But you don't have any *evidence* about Trot and this judge's wife! That's why it's so dangerous.'

Ray smiled. 'There's a man called Elliott Standing. He's number two in the Lord Chancellor's office and I met him when the Circuit judges and their wives came here. Standing was up from London sniffing out who should be tried as assistant recorders or put on the Circuit bench. He stayed to dinner afterwards and just before midnight he got a taxi back to the King's Arms – .'

'And after you'd poured a gallon of brandy down him,' Helen added tartly. 'Is that the man?'

'He did have a few,' admitted her husband, 'but Standing whispered something to me. He said he'd seen Trot pawing "No-Knickers". That's Mrs Anona Chandelle-Sweet's nickname.'

'When did he see that?'

'Recently.'

'He might have been patting her on the back,' suggested Helen, ever charitable.

'On the front apparently.' Ray was grinning now.

'Trotter did this in his room at the Lords?'

'In his flat upstairs. Standing took something up for him and the door was open.'

Helen thought for a moment. 'But (a) Standing was drunk when he told you. And in any case . . .' Helen was one of those people who annoyed Ray by never going on to (b), leaving it hanging there like the man upstairs who drops one shoe on the floor. 'In any case, would he repeat the allegation if it came to the crunch?'

'Helen, one has to assume that barristers who work in the office of the Lord Chancellor have a certain integrity,' said Ray piously.

'I hope you're right, Ray.' Helen was a worried woman now – a good deal more worried than she showed.

The Lord Chancellor's panelled room in the House of Lords end of the Palace of Westminster was on the floor below his flat. It looked on to that great river, the Thames, still flowing as it had done from distant days when curious foreign invaders paddled along it, nosing into its creeks and marshes. However Lord Chancellor Trotter was not admiring the view. Instead he was in serious discussion with his permanent secretary, puffy studious-looking Anthony Halesworth Kingston KCB.

Sir Anthony was a more powerful person than he looked. The Lord Chancellor had a busy life presiding over the House of Lords, sitting in the Cabinet and even acting as a judge in the House of Lords – odd for a government minister, and only defensible, like so much in Britain, because it had always been so and no-one was daring enough to question it. This was Ray Slingsby's opinion at any rate. So it was the Lord Chancellor's permanent secretary and his underlings who collected information on candidates for judgeships.

The decision to appoint was in most cases that of the civil servant. It was merely rubber-stamped by the Lord Chancellor, who scrawled his signature or initials against names put before him. In fact the Lord Chancellor never met most judges until they were sworn-in before him in that panelled room. This made the permanent secretary a very important person, and the job required someone of the highest calibre and integrity.

On paper Sir Anthony Kingston KCB was just that. After Eton he had read Greats – Latin, Greek and ancient history and philosophy – at Balliol College, Oxford, gaining a double first. Success in Greats guaranteed greatness; such was the theory hallowed by centuries. Kingston was also good at cricket, having captained Eton and gained a blue at Oxford. Success in the fields of Classics and cricket had long been an entree into the law.

However, Kingston failed to build a practice in his four years at the Bar, though his failure was mentioned by none and known to few. His ambition had been the High Court bench, like his uncle, Lord Justice Kingston, and his grandfather, Law Lord Kingston of Norbiton, but it never occurred to Tony that the family's forensic genius was being diluted generation by generation. At the cocktail-parties that he so enjoyed – socially he was somebody – he never admitted that opting for the security of the civil service denoted failure. 'I decided that appointing judges was preferable to being one,' he would say with the fluent self-confidence instilled by Eton college, founded by Henry II for poor scholars of whom Anthony Halesworth Kingston had, in theory, been one.

'The sodomite has to be stopped.'

The permanent secretary's eyes narrowed for an instant at this statement by Lord Trotter. It could have reflected on his own sexual preference, though surely not – nobody in his public life knew, so far as he was aware. So many prominent gays had come out or had been 'outed' that he sometimes wondered if it mattered anyway? In his job it did, though. He carried his burden of guilt secretly, furtively, as he had since Eton. His rent-boys were a separate part of his life, and he was careful to keep it that way.

'There are certain difficulties, Lord Chancellor,' said Sir Anthony smoothly.

'I'm aware of that,' snapped Trotter.

'By what is now the Supreme Court Act 1981, a High Court judge . . .'

'I know, Kingston, I know.' The man's a pedantic fool, thought the Lord Chancellor.

Undeterred, his permanent secretary spelt out the problem, 'A High Court judge can only be dismissed if both Houses of Parliament vote to do so, and that has never happened.'

'All right Kingston, you've made it perfectly clear. Now let *me* make it clear that Mr Justice Fucking Slingsby has to be destroyed.'

Kingston gulped. 'Er – destroyed, Lord Chancellor?'

'Yes, and by *you.*'

'Does that come within my terms of employment, sir?'

'Yes.' Trotter's tone brooked no opposition.

Kingston felt that his master's sordid and devious train of thought seemed to have left the rails. But where, he wondered, was it heading?

'I understand your concern, Lord Chancellor, and indeed all of us here share it, I am sure. Mr Justice Slingsby, no doubt with the best of motives, as he sees it . . .'

'You can cut out the cant, Kingston.'

Kingston felt as he did when he was 'vivaed' at Oxford – questioned by dons who had to decide whether to give him a first. He'd waffled his way through then, so surely he could do it again. He had more experience of life now.

He tried again. 'Undesirable as Mr Justice Slingsby's public statements have been, especially as reflecting on your own integrity, and indeed on mine, on all of us here at the centre of the system . . .'

'For God's sake, man.' Lord Trotter glared at him menacingly.

Kingston didn't think his efforts were succeeding. One last try. 'Lord Chancellor, if it comes to the point . . .'

'I wish *you* would, Kingston.'

'Parliament – it has to be both Houses – they may not see Mr Justice Slingsby's conduct, er, misconduct, as we do.'

'Who said anything about Parliament yet?'

'But, Lord Chancellor, there's no other way ...'

Lord Trotter spoke slowly, as if to an idiot. 'The ground has to be prepared first.'

The permanent secretary felt the ground was still giving way under him. 'Naturally, Lord Chancellor, whatever I can do ...'

'And you'd better be quick, Kingston. Because if anything happens to me in all this – and it could – I shan't be the only one to go.'

'I don't quite see, Lord Chancellor.'

'I know you don't. All that first class honours stuff – no guarantee of common sense, eh?'

What could Kingston say to that? But he couldn't sit silent while Lord Trotter stared at him in that threatening way. He tried to pull his mind into shape. 'A plan of campaign is called for, do you think, Lord Chancellor?'

Lord Trotter thumped the desk between them with his fist, making the papers on it bounce. 'You realise the man has even had the nerve to hint, more than hint, that there's something wrong between me and Mrs Chandelle-Sweet.'

'A disgraceful allegation. He must be made to withdraw it, nothing less.' Kingston tried to sound as determined as his master.

'But a lot, lot more,' snorted Trotter, 'though you don't seem able to see it, Kingston. That man has suggested impropriety between me and my private secretary, and all you suggest is that he *withdraws* it?'

'You could sue him,' was the tentative suggestion.

29

'Now you *are* being daft. The Lord Chancellor going before a High Court judge and jury to sue another High Court judge? Can you imagine what the tabloids would make of that? The *Sun*, the *Mirror* and that new one – what's it called, the *Courier*? My reputation would never recover. To suggest that me and my secretary . . . ' Lord Trotter looked sharply at the civil servant. 'What do *you* think about it, Kingston?'

Kingston's mind leapt. It could have won a Gold at the Olympic Mental High Jump, if they had one. Was he really being asked what he thought about Trot and No-Knickers? He hadn't actually witnessed their coital embrace, but he had a pretty good idea what had been going on upstairs – perhaps even enough to satisfy a civil court on the balance of probabilities, though probably not a jury on the basis of beyond reasonable doubt. He had his number two's word for the embrace, but Lord Trotter would probably (a) deny it, or (b) say he was *fastening* the button on her blouse and not *un*-fastening it. Confessing and avoiding was the legal term.

Lord Trotter was getting impatient. 'Well, what *do* you think, Kingston?'

'I think we shall have to do something.' He knew it was feeble before he said it. It was so feeble that Trot didn't even bother to acknowledge it.

'I was hoping, Kingston, to confer silk on you when the list of new QCs comes out next Easter.'

Kingston tried to pretend he didn't hear the

implied threat. 'I've already compiled the list, Lord Chancellor,' he said hopefully.

'Is your name on it?'

Kingston looked shocked. 'Oh no, sir. Certainly not.'

'Well, if it is, you can erase it now.'

The threat had materialised. Oh dear.

Watching his permanent secretary's crushed face, Lord Trotter went on, 'For the time being, at any rate. You must understand these things aren't entirely automatic. Anyone who gets silk from me has to earn it.'

This was a new one on Kingston, but he didn't think it politic to say so.

'And don't forget, permanent secretaries can be retired for limited efficiency, eh?'

This was too much for Kingston. 'Well, actually no, Lord Chancellor. If you look at regulation . . .'

'Bugger the small print, Kingston. Let me spell it out. You and I have got to see off that sod Slingsby before he sees *us* off, so you'd better get your thinking-cap on. I'll give you three days to come up with something. And don't argue or I'll make it less.'

Kingston bowed to the inevitable. 'I shall devote all my time to it, Lord Chancellor. Every second.' He would have preferred the interview to end here, but there was another, related, matter, which he had to bring to his master's attention.

'Lord Chancellor, the *Courier* want to know what Judge Chandelle-Sweet's track-record as a barrister is. They say have we tried him out as assistant recorder? That does usually happen, as I know you're well aware.'

'That's all right in theory, Kingston, but the shortage – you know how short we are of judges, good judges.'

'Quite so, Lord Chancellor.' Kingston didn't think it tactful to say that according to his file Chandelle-Sweet didn't seem to have been good at anything he had ever done.

'When he came for interview, I thought he was quite impressive,' Lord Trotter said, making a lame attempt to explain the inexplicable.

Kingston struggled with his conscience. He remembered Sir Robert Armstrong's famous phrase. How economical with the truth could a permanent secretary be?

'You told me Sweet would be all right on the bench eventually,' the Lord Chancellor said.

'Did I?'

'Didn't you write it down, Kingston?'

'Certainly not.' Kingston had long since learnt that the only things a sensible senior civil servant writes down and enters in a file are those things that will do him some good if they are ever disinterred.

'Anyway,' the Lord Chancellor steamrollered on, 'I had to make a decision and it's too late to alter it now. We've got to defend Sweet's appointment. So get into that office of yours and get your thinking-cap on, or we're both going to be well and truly in the fertiliser. Eh, Kingston?'

2

HIS HONOUR Judge Alwyne Chandelle-Sweet, fully robed except for his wig, sat in his room at Willesden County Court during an adjournment of the civil action *Harrison v Assorted Biscuits*. A weedy, nervous-looking man in his late forties, he was not an impressive sight, especially when, as now, he was trying to relax.

His small feet were propped up on the old desk. In one hand he held a cigar and in the other a cup of coffee – Irish, though the usher who had brought it did not know that. The judge always carried a small flask to fortify himself against the rigours of the day. After generous use of its contents, he would admit to himself that some of the day's rigours would be almost too much for him without it.

That day's *Courier* lay open on the desk. Alwyne had read the story about Mr Justice Slingsby's speech to the magistrates, but frankly he couldn't make head or tail of it. It seemed to refer to him: to accuse him of something, but he couldn't make out what. After all, the only thing he had done was

33

accept an appointment to the bench made by the Lord Chancellor, who had at last recognised his ability.

He was baffled by the reference to his wife Anona, the Lord Chancellor's private secretary. What was she supposed to have done wrong? She hadn't done anything except serve her boss faithfully, daily giving all she had, as any good employee should. He tried to read through the press report again, but threw it aside in disgust. What could you expect, he thought, of a paper clearly designed to titillate the unwashed, illiterate and insane?

Maybe it was the wine he'd drunk the previous evening. He'd lost count of the bottles he had helped to empty as a guest at the Bar mess. This was where the barristers met every month, and the set amount that they paid for the evening included as much wine as they wanted, so everyone got as sloshed as they could.

He had been the guest of honour, to celebrate his recent appointment. How nice of them. Some of his barrister colleagues had gone out of their way to say kind things about him, which they had never done before. The leader of the Circuit had made a brilliant speech, very witty as usual, saying they all knew that Alwyne would adhere to the standard with which they were all familiar, and that no doubt the Court of Appeal would be kept busy.

Everybody fell about laughing, and Alwyne joined in though he wasn't sure what the joke was. But it was good to go to the Bar mess; everyone let their hair down and he hoped they would invite him regularly.

What great times they'd had in the past. There was the occasion when, to general merriment, Ellis Greetley had taken the piano apart and couldn't put it together again. Unfortunately the club hadn't seen the point of the pile of black and white ivories and pieces of wood, and had sent a large bill, but somebody had paid after they had received a solicitor's letter. Great fun.

And then there was the time Christopher Hangham QC slid down the bannisters, forgetting there was a knob at the bottom. He had never worked again after that, in court or in bed, and was in hospital for six months, but it was a great laugh on the night and they often talked about it. Such great characters, barristers.

It was a good thing the local constabulary were so friendly, thought Alwyne, because many a member of the mess had narrow escapes on the way home. One QC, later a Law Lord, was stopped by the police while driving his car along the near-side pavement. When he got out he fell flat on his face in the gutter, but the understanding man in blue merely helped him back in his car and walked away, saying, 'Good night sir. Mind how you go.'

No, people who criticised barristers only knew half the story: they were a grand lot, most of them. But some had been a bit unkind to Alwyne at the Bar, and by jove they'd get their come-uppance when they did cases in his court now.

The usher came in to say that the court was

ready to resume. Alwyne, finding it difficult to gather what *Harrison v Assorted Biscuits* was about, had announced a quarter-of-an-hour adjournment to let the expert consulting engineer Dr Henry S. Fosgitt, have a breather. Alwyne believed in frequent adjournments – they were only fair to counsel and expert witnesses, who were all paid by the day. Now he told the usher they could have another ten minutes.

Usher George Beaver, a man of eighty-two, had long ago retired from the police force and almost from life itself. His eyes always brimmed with stagnant water and there was a permanent drop on the end of his nose. He was deaf and usually got everything wrong, but ushers weren't paid much. George was glad of the work and nobody had the heart to sack him – it would kill him, all agreed.

Alwyne looked at the case papers. The Particulars of Claim and Defence were supplemented by lengthy requests for further and better particulars and replies: pages and pages of them. Some counsel did so well out of drafting such unnecessary documents that they made a good living though they hardly ever appeared in court. Alwyne had never found civil actions easy to grasp and though at first sight this case seemed straightforward, it wasn't.

Six years ago the plaintiff had been at work at his machine in the Assorted Biscuits factory. Biscuits came from the machine on some sort of conveyor-belt – there were photographs. It was the plaintiff's duty to ensure that the biscuits did not get jammed as they emerged on to the belt.

On the morning in question he was having his tea at 10 o'clock – a girl brought the tea round while the factory hands continued to work at their machines. A biscuit, or part of a biscuit, lodged in his throat, causing him to cough uncontrollably, the Particulars of Claim alleged. In consequence of which the defendant caused or permitted his left knee to come into contact with a metal part of the machine which obtruded by three inches, thereby fracturing his knee-cap.

The alleged breaches of duty were very complicated, because the regulations under the Factories Act were very complicated. It wasn't even clear to Alwyne whether the offending biscuit had been one the plaintiff was eating at the time, or whether it had in some way jumped off the belt and into his mouth. He daren't ask counsel, in case they laughed at him for missing something obvious. It would all come out in the wash, he hoped.

But the medical reports were so detailed and difficult, and the disabilities the plaintiff alleged to have flowed from the lodging of the offending biscuit in his throat, were astonishing. He could no longer eat or cough normally, was kept awake at night, had lost confidence in himself, had a nervous breakdown, tried three times to commit suicide and had been unable to play football with his nine-year-old son.

How on earth could all that be sorted out in terms of damages? The only safe thing in the end, Alwyne thought, might be to find for the defendants, and then he would not have to assess damages. That would be sad, because the plaintiff looked a nice man, and he had only been doing his job. Nobody said he'd been larking about or throwing biscuits around.

No, *Harrison v Assorted Biscuits* was not going to be easy, Alwyne told himself, reluctantly draining his coffee cup and reaching for his wig. He had already asked if he could only try criminal cases, but the courts administrator had only said he'd think about it. How he wished now he had a nice simple robbery with violence to deal with instead of this.

Alwyne had been christened Alan, in the days when his parents were still called Candle. Little Alan – he was a puny child – was born in a semi-detached council house. His father Albert was then a police constable, but soon after Alan's birth he was compelled to leave the force when falsely accused of shop-lifting. It was all some muddle, of course, and he did not appear in court, though he still had to resign.

After that he set up a security firm with another police constable who'd had to leave the force suddenly. The firm prospered, but after a time there was another misunderstanding when police officers, who had known Albert in the force and were jealous of his success, said he had given information to burglars about a warehouse where he had fitted alarms.

The Crown Prosecution Service and chief constable agreed not to prosecute Albert Candle if he left the security firm and undertook in writing not to be engaged in another such firm for ten years. Albert was reluctant – he knew they hadn't much to go on except the burglars' own evidence – but he had eventually agreed when his co-director had paid him a substantial sum for his shares. Albert then went into metal-grinding with a man he'd once unsuccessfully interviewed on a charge of fraud. They did so well that when Alan was ten he was sent to Rainwater, a preparatory school in North Yorkshire. He was entered under the name Alwyne Chandelle-Sweet – his parents had adopted the new surname by deed poll. They thought the name Candle was too pedestrian. It would throw insufficient light on the promising path that they were determined their son should take in life. Young Alwyne, as he must now be called, had to speak posh and look posh and then he'd do a lot better than they had. In spite of their money and their change of name, it was too late for the elder Chandelle-Sweets to make it socially. The right people would never accept them now, but where they had failed they were determined for their son to succeed.

It was sheer chance that sent Alwyne to Rainwater. When involved in one of his shady business deals, Albert happened to meet a man who had a son there. The deal had to do with getting metal-grinding equipment from East Germany to the UK without offending the laws of either country – in fact without the officials of either country knowing anything about it at all.

The boys at Rainwater school had two rules, which they enforced rigidly. The first was never be cheeky to one's seniors – seniority being determined not by age but by date of going to the school. The second was never be rude about another boy's parents. This reflected the extremely mixed nature of the school's intake.

Alwyne broke both rules within weeks of his arrival at the bleak establishment, thus condemning himself to a wide range of punishments. These varied from being suspended from a tree in the orchard by his ankles for an hour each day for a week, to being sent to Coventry for two weeks. He preferred the tree, being a sociable boy who genuinely wanted to get on with his peers.

Happily, Alwyne was not the brightest of boys. His brain burnt slowly and with an uncertain flame. Being bright would have caused added resentment from his contemporaries, increasing his misery. The boy prosecutors and judges at Rainwater were not bright, though many were highly polished to listen to – just like life in the law, as Alwyne later discovered.

The one thing Alwyne did well at Rainwater, and it was a very important thing, was playing rugger. Small, nippy and quick, he made a surprisingly good wing. If Rainwater was famous for anything, it was for the success of its rugger teams. Soccer, on the other hand, was strictly forbidden in the school, and anyone seen kicking a round ball was subject to draconian punishment by the head, Togger Tatham.

At eighteen, Togger had been an England trialist at Twickers and had scored three tries. He never earned an England cap, but those three tries carried him triumphantly onwards through life, via a rugger scholarship to Brasenose College, Oxford, where he would have gained a blue had not an over-suspicious constable misinterpreted his presence in a public lavatory.

He was not sent down, but slid down to an obscure polytechnic where he managed to obtain a BA – without honours – followed by a teaching qualification. In reality he was qualified for little beyond rugger and the buggery of little boys, who were plentiful at Rainwater. Alwyne Chandelle-Sweet was one of Togger's aptest and most compliant pupils, and the headmaster had no hesitation in recommending him to Dramlingham, a minor public school in West Yorkshire. Togger was as sad to see the back of Alwyne when he left Rainwater as he had been glad to see it all the time he was there.

The usher knocked again. Alwyne told him that he would knock on the door to the bench in a few moments, when he had finished perusing the case papers. He picked up the *Courier* again. What a vile slanderer that socialist Slingsby was. He had heard they called his dear wife Anona No-Knickers behind her slender back, but it was a disgusting slur. The only time her Valley of Delight was not protected by these undergarments was when he lay beside her warm and ample form by night, or when by day she was moved to sudden passion beyond his normal ration and they had it off on the drawing-room carpet.

41

Sadly, Anona's passionate moments were very rare now, but when they came they still had the power to flatter his ego and inflame, sometimes even inflate, his prick. Thank goodness that since leaving Dramlingham he had put buggery behind him. He rarely looked at a boy in that shameful way any longer, and if he did he was able to resist the temptation. Except on one or two occasions recently when he had been drunk at parties, and they didn't count.

Alwyne didn't blame his wife for being less ardent these days. She was no longer as young as she had been when he married her twelve years ago, and her prestigious job with that much maligned man Lord Trotter took a lot out of her.

Alwyne now bitterly regretted that a few months ago, while drunk, he had accused Anona of having it off with Trotter. Great men didn't do that sort of thing, he should have realised, and the Lord Chancellor was a great man. He must be, since he was the first person in authority since Togger Tatham ever to recognise Alwyne's talent.

People said Trot was thick and insensitive, 'graceless and faceless,' according to *Private Eye*. Few had a good word for him, yet Alwyne thought he might aptly be called a colossus. Trot had actually sent for him, invited him to a face-to-face interview. In his previous applications to sit as assistant recorder Alwyne had never progressed beyond snooty civil servants.

The file they had on him, as on most barristers,

must hold better reports than Alwyne had thought; not that he had seen the file or would want to. Open government had to have limits. It would not do to let ordinary people know too much about their governors' doings – it would lower respect for them. And it would be communism wouldn't it, or would it? Socialism then. Not that he knew the difference – left was left and never in the right, so far as he was concerned.

Alwyne's butterfly mind flitted back to Trotter. How very, very decisive and daring to make him a judge without even trying him out as assistant recorder for a single day. Alwyne would never let that wonderful man down, and he was sure Anona would never let Lord Trotter down either. However much he might pile work on top of her, Alwyne was sure she would grit her teeth and get through it. What a good woman he was privileged to be married to; angelic even.

He looked at his watch. He must, he really must go back into court and face that appalling Factory Act case. He would try to be courageous and ask how the biscuit was supposed to have arrived in the unfortunate plaintiff's throat. But first another glance at the *Courier*. They were desperately trying to outdo the *Sun*, he thought. The *Courier* had even gone so far as to attack Her Majesty the Queen, saying that Buckingham Palace was far too big for one family, and that she should open it to the general public as a heritage fun park. What treacherous impudence! Nothing was too bad for such scribblers of sewage. They would destroy

43

everything great in Great Britain, if they could, just like that viper Raymond Slingsby.

A tap on the door to the bench.

'Come in.'

George Beaver came in, so diffidently that he could have been about to fall to his knees and pray.

'Your honour. The clerk has asked me to say – they *are* ready and it's nearly twelve o'clock.' The drop fell from his nose and he wiped it from his trousers with his hand.

'And so am I ready, of course. I was waiting for you.'

'But your honour, you said . . .'

'No no. Don't apologise.' Alwyne drew himself to his full five feet six inches. Into battle, he thought, as the usher led the way on to the bench.

'Silence in court. All stand.'

His Honour Judge Alwyne Chandelle-Sweet was about to resume the case of *Harrison v Assorted Biscuits*. He would decide it with all the dignity, authority and knowledge he possessed. To the untutored it would not look too bad.

The judge slipped as he reached the large chair on the bench. Groping for the support of the arms, he settled into it uncertainly. He should have known the Irish coffee would be a mistake on top of last night's red wine. As Alwyne looked down at the barrister who was on his feet already, eager to resume, he had difficulty in making out his face. Surely his eyesight wasn't as bad as that, was it?

The Channel 6 TV programme was in the series

`Currant Affairs', a title so clever that not even the producer Jonathan Hebble understood it. However, he hesitated to query it, bearing in mind recent redundancies. The presenter this week was Janet Yorke, a freelance journalist from Barfield, who admitted to being twenty-nine, but was in fact thirty-two. She was a dark, handsome, high-cheekboned, bluntly spoken, gritty, self-confident product of state education and Barfield university. On leaving university she had gone into newspaper journalism with the intention of becoming a second Jean Rook. Now that she worked in television she had substituted Esther Rantzen as her model, though she lacked the hearty manner and the teeth.

As a foot-in-door local newspaper reporter, Janet had always dug out the facts, however unpalatable, and presented them palatably to her news editor. Then she took her investigative skills to TV – an upward career move, she had hoped, though she seemed to have become stuck on the present rung of ambition's ladder. Even so, Janet's bricklayer father would have been proud of her, had they not stopped speaking more than ten years ago when she had insisted on obtaining the higher education that he despised, not having had it himself.

Janet had much to give TV: an earnest manner and looks that make-up could do wonders with in the hour she always insisted on. She had the sexiness that all male TV producers looked for in women presenters and some, including Jonathan, insisted on sampling. He had Janet once a week coincidentally with the programme. He was married; she was a childless divorcee. She also had a mortgage in arrears on her Barfield flat, for Janet had one quality inherited from her feckless father: she always spent more than she earned.

Janet was presenting this edition of 'Currant Affairs' from Channel 6's London studio. In the studio with her she had a very nervous Judge Chandelle-Sweet, who was by no means sure what he was doing there, and the Right Honourable Lord Trotter, Lord Chancellor. The Honourable Mr Justice Slingsby was in the TV station's Barfield studio. Both the latter two were a good deal more confident than their sweating colleague.

'This evening is a rare and welcome occasion,' began Janet, looking earnestly into the camera. 'Until quite recently judges were never seen or heard in public outside their courtrooms. But a wind of change is sweeping through our courts of justice. And to discuss the latest developments we have, here in London, Lord Chancellor Trotter who heads the legal system and appoints all judges, and Circuit Judge Alwyne Chandelle-Sweet, whose appointment has caused a certain amount of comment. In our Barfield studio is Mr Justice Raymond Slingsby, who has been the centre of the recent press and radio controversy about judicial appointments.'

She turned to Lord Trotter. 'Lord Chancellor, what do you have to say about recent press criticism of yourself?'

'Never read the tabloids,' snapped Lord Trotter.

'Not newspapers at all. Comics for kids. Garbage.'

'But the *Courier* alone sells over two million copies, and the *Sun* well over . . .'

Lord Trotter's eyes bulged. 'Don't mention the *Sun*. A running sewer, written by sewer-rats.'

Janet smiled slightly. 'Well that's frank, Lord Chancellor. But could it be libellous, possibly?'

'Don't you mean slander, young lady?' Lord Trotter looked pleased with himself. He had scored a point, he thought.

'No, libel,' chipped in Slingsby, who was listening through his earpiece. Unfortunately, the monitor in the Barfield studio didn't give him a proper view of what was going on in London, but he could imagine that bastard Trotter's smug expression, and was determined not to let him get away with it. That girl presenter sounded as though she had her head screwed on properly, he thought. She had a nice voice and he wondered if she was pretty, but from where he was sitting she was just a coloured blur.

'It's broadcasting and that's a statutory exception. As most lawyers know,' Slingsby continued. He gave the camera in front of him what he hoped was a meaningful look.

Fascinating though this was, Janet reluctantly decided they were being sidetracked. 'But to return to my original question, Lord Chancellor, do you have anything to say to your critics on judicial appointments?'

'No.' Lord Trotter's expression was mulish.

'Nothing at all?' coaxed Janet.

He glared defiantly out at the audience, his face

redder than ever. 'If you want me to spell it out, they haven't the faintest idea what they're talking about.'

The camera cut to a close-up of Slingsby's reaction. He was clearly dying to speak and Janet gave him his head. 'Do come in, Judge.'

'Lord Trotter,' said Raymond Slingsby, politely but firmly, 'is talking codswallop. It's all wrong, one man deciding who shall be judges. There should be a committee, as there is in every other supposedly civilised country.'

Back to the Lord Chancellor. 'The best committee is a committee of one. In this case, that happens to be me.'

Slingsby could not contain himself. 'But how can you be sure?' He looked directly at the camera. 'It has been said that the present incumbent is the worst Lord Chancellor this century.'

In the London studio, a speechless Lord Trotter was trying to look as if this remark was beneath his notice and failing badly. This was great stuff, thought Janet. 'Do go on, judge,' she urged, but Slingsby had lobbed his grenade.

'There's nothing more to say. Except that you seem to have forgotten about His Honour Judge Alwyne Chandelle-Sweet, and it's his shocking appointment that's at the root of it all.'

Alwyne attempted a brave smile as Janet turned to him. 'Judge Chandelle-Sweet? Would you care to comment?'

'Shocking? It's er, it's, er, it hasn't shocked me,' Alwyne stuttered. 'I'm finding it a ... challenge. Not easy, but ...'

Slingsby pounced. 'It's too much for him. He's not up to it.'

Alwyne looked hurt. 'I may not be as clever as Mr Justice Slingsby, but there's no need for him to be gratitudinally rude.'

Slingsby smiled. 'You see. He can't even speak English properly.'

'I *am* up to the job,' insisted Alwyne petulantly.

Furious, the Lord Chancellor butted in. 'Of course he is. No question. This is simply an attempt to humiliate the judiciary by Mr Justice Slingsby, who certainly shouldn't be on the bench himself. I didn't appoint him. Socialist riff-raff.'

'I don't care how long the Lord Chancellor goes on blustering,' said Slingsby calmly, 'but I can assure him I have no intention of resigning.'

The producer was making frantic noises to Janet. She knew it was time to get to the heart of the matter. 'Judge, you told the magistrates that the appointment of Judge Chandelle-Sweet may have a certain ulterior motive. What precisely are you saying was wrong with it?'

'I shall sue, I warn you,' bellowed the Lord Chancellor.

Slingsby ignored him. 'Judge Sweet has no talent for the law in any way that I or anyone else has ever noticed. So why did Lord Trotter put him on the bench? Is his relationship with the judge's wife behind it?'

Janet's eyes gleamed. Now he was finally going to commit himself on camera. This would be a major coup. 'But *what* relationship, Mr Justice Slingsby?'

She was to be disappointed. 'I shall be addressing the magistrates at Chesterfield one week from today,' said Slingsby. 'And I intend to be specific.'

'The damages'll be enormous,' howled Lord Trotter, beside himself with rage.

'Not if it's true,' said Slingsby firmly. 'And it will be.'

The producer was making noises again. Time was almost up. Janet heaved a small sigh of disappointment. Still, what they had already would be great television. 'And we shall all wait to hear from you with very great interest, Mr Justice Slingsby. Thank you, and thank you, Lord Chancellor, for being so refreshingly frank. So, there is a wind of change in the legal profession, and next week there will be a change of subject – Is lesbianism better for your health than sodomy? Now back to the studio . . .'

Tough, hard-faced little Harry Minnor sat grimacing at one of the dozen TV sets at No. 10 Downing Street. One had to keep abreast of what was going on, however distasteful. But things were getting out of hand, he thought to himself ruefully. As Prime Minister he had openly espoused Open Government and Freedom of Information. They weren't as important now the election was over, but they had helped substantially in winning yet another victory for the party, the natural party of government, which – in the interest of the nation and certainly of Tory MPs who formed its backbone always and its

50

funny-bone sometimes – had to remain in power indefinitely. Democracy demanded it. The people wanted it. The press – the best parts of it – accepted it and he, Harry Minnor, was certain the nation needed the Tory party because, apart from other considerations, he liked his job.

It was so much better than driving a No. 9 bus – though No. 10 too had its hazards and collisions. He preferred prime ministering to piloting a jumbo-jet, to which he had graduated from bus-driving until grounded for momentarily forgetting which switch let down the landing-wheels. Anyone could make a mistake like that, though the Saudi-Arabian ambassador, one of the distinguished passengers aboard, had not thought it amusing to be ejected prematurely on to the tarmac down the emergency chute, his robes awry and his head-dress removed.

There had been an angry debate at the UN about the incident, initiated by the Saudi delegate and based on the proposition that nobody seemed to like the Arabs. It went on so long and became so heated that the cause of it all – the unfortunate grounding of flight AB982 – was overlooked. The official enquiry reported two and a half years later that mechanical malfunction was the most likely cause of the accident. However, as the black box had mysteriously been lost while in transit, no one would ever be certain, and anyway by the time the enquiry result was known Harry Minnor had forsaken the cool air of the stratosphere for the warmer and more feet-on-the-ground atmosphere of Westminster.

He had been selected as Tory candidate for the safe Labour seat of Greater Snotting in mid-Lancashire, where his appeal to the electors varied according to his audience. In speaking to Tory women he emphasised law and order and said, 'We need less of soft soap and more of the rope,' which was interpreted by some as a call for the return of capital punishment. When criticized by the local Tory Reform Group, Harry Minnor said 'rope' meant 'skipping rope' and that he was talking about a local children's playgroup – which had ample cloakroom facilities but not enough toys.

The *Snotting Gazette* – a newspaper with dangerous Liberal Democratic tendencies – accused Harry of inconsistencies. His reply was delivered at a meeting of Alcoholics Anonymous on an evening when he had dined well beforehand at a local inn. When raising the subject of 'inconsistencies', he made four attempts to say the word, then gave up, substituted 'lies', hiccupped twice and nearly fell over. This went down well with AA members, several of whom rushed forward offering him application forms for membership. When the incident was reported in the *Gazette*, frequenters of the Snotting Arms and other hostelries felt that here at last was a candidate who was truly one of them, and the large pub vote immediately swung to Harry.

To the members of Snotting Working Men's Club, Harry hinted that the mishap at London airport was really part of his campaign against the Arabs and any other wogs who dared show disrespect to the Union Jack and the Royal Family. Analysed, this lacked logic, but no-one did analyse it and the resultant pandemonium brought the local police to the hall. Thinking that the revolution had at last broken out and that they would be the first to go, the police went discreetly back to police headquarters, reporting that it was merely an enthusiastic political meeting. This was a rare instance of the police telling the truth by accident.

Harry Minnor won the seat, turning a Labour majority of 12,872 into a Tory one of 1,064, the largest swing in the country. This marked him out as a man to watch, and he was soon junior minister at the Department of Health. From then on his rise was unstoppable, culminating in his appointment as Foreign Secretary. This was surprisingly successful, in view of the fact that foreign affairs bored him rigid, but Harry had by now perfected the art of delegation and left everything to his civil servants, highly intelligent men and women who could see all sides to every question. This meant that nothing was ever decided, so no policies were ever implemented and nothing could go wrong. After that, when the office of Prime Minister fell vacant just before the election, he was clearly the only man for the job.

That damned TV programme, thought Harry as he sat watching the news without taking it in (they were talking about South Africa, where he thought the blacks were quite well enough treated without lavishing the vote on them). What were those bewigged idiots thinking of? For centuries judges had kept as silent as Trappist monks and now they were running around opening their mouths to anyone who would listen. No wonder they called the Lord Chancellor 'Trot': the man had the brains of a horse.

Harry would have preferred Eustace Fothergill QC on the Woolsack, but the Cabinet wouldn't let him make the appointment. They said Fothergill was too left-wing, which in a barrister who called himself a Tory was as good as saying he was ready for the funny farm. Harry didn't think it at all amusing to be over-ruled by a Cabinet he had himself selected, but one had to consult one's colleagues in such small matters, to preserve the pretence that they were still a democracy and not a Thatcherite one-party dictatorship.

The Cabinet consensus was that the Buggins's Turn rule could not be flouted and as Trotter was elected an MP six months before Fothergill, Trotter was senior and that was that. Seniority was important, and long service had to have its rewards. Otherwise who would endure all that dreadful sitting around late at night, waiting to make a speech that would be listened to by no-one save nodding Hansard reporters, a slumbering Speaker and a handful of MPs who muttered, glared and pointed to their watches?

The PM had had enough of the Lord Chancellor's boorishness and lack of tact. They were surplus qualifications for sitting on the Woolsack. Woolsack, he mused. What did that bag of wool symbolise? He betted no one knew, but it had been there so long, the contents compressed by dozens of corpulent Lord Chancellors, the cover worn thin. Was it really wool in there, even? Suppose they looked inside and found it wasn't. Probably find it was made in Taiwan, given the state of the country's industry. He pulled himself up with a jerk. This wouldn't do. He must speak to Trotter right away.

Lord Trotter was in the Channel 6 hospitality room, relaxing. He was chatting confidentially to a production assistant with big tits, and taking advantage of the free-flowing wine, even though it was Algerian. When the message came from the Prime Minister, he abandoned his glass unfinished – something he had never done before in his life. A short while later he was knocking hesitantly on the door of the Harry Minnor's study upstairs at No. 10.

'Oswald, old chap, dear friend.'

The familiarity sounded ominous. The PM was only as friendly as that when about to bollock you, at the very least.

'Yes, PM.'

'Call me Harry. It's time you did.' This was even worse. 'I wanted to talk to you about that TV programme you were on this evening.'

Trot's fears were suddenly multiplied. It was as if he'd stepped on the accelerator instead of the brake, something that did happen to the Lord Chancellor from time to bibulous time. Thank heavens for our wonderful police once they recognised who you were.

'Was it wise, do you think, to go on TV at all?'

That was a fast one – so fast that Trotter hit out

at it blindly. 'Well, it seemed a good idea at the time.' He laughed in a feeble way.

Harry did not laugh. 'It was a mistake.'

'Yes, PM, er . . . Harry,' said Trot submissively.

'It must not happen again, not without my express permission. Next time, get my permission in writing first.' The Prime Minister gave him a hard look. 'If there *is* a next time. You've got yourself into a hell of a bloody muddle. The tabloids are full of it. Even the broadsheets are on to it now. Did you see the leader in the *Guardian*?'

Trot was offended. 'I don't read the *Guardian*. There's been nothing in *The Times*.'

'You wait. But I'm not prepared to, Oswald. Slingsby says he's going to blow the gaff on you in one week's time. What are you going to do about it?'

'Deny it,' said the Lord Chancellor in a sullen voice. He was being made to feel like a naughty schoolboy and he didn't like it.

'But the man has evidence, obviously.'

Trotter looked mutinous. 'We'll have to see what it is, sir, won't we?'

'Are you out of what mind you have, Oswald? Slingsby doesn't look like a bullshitter to me, so just explain how you're going to stop the balloon going up?'

'If you should happen to have any suggestions, Prime Minister.' He couldn't bring himself to call him Harry under the circumstances.

'You've got to shut Mr Justice Slingsby up once and for all,' said Harry Minnor firmly.

Trotter cheered up a little. 'I'm glad to hear you

say that, PM. So you agree on drastic measures?'

'Essential.'

'He will be attended to, I assure you sir. Drastically.'

Minnor gave him a suspicious look. 'You're not going to have him done in, I hope?'

'It shouldn't be necessary.'

'It had better not be,' said Minnor. 'Think what the *Courier* would make of it. "Lord Chancellor has Judge murdered."'

'No.' Trotter couldn't help himself. '"Law boss slays Judge."'

'I thought you never read the tabloids, Oswald.'

Was the PM actually being humorous? His face didn't so much as flicker. 'And don't forget, Oswald, Eustace Fothergill's practice at the Bar isn't going too well. That last libel case of his, the woman the *Courier* said went about without knickers. Remember?'

Trot's heart missed several beats. What was he hinting? Did he know about Anona?

'Eustace fell asleep during the summing-up,' the PM went on.

Trotter leapt to the defence of his colleague. 'It can happen. You'd be surprised how often.'

'But Oswald, most barristers don't start sleep-walking, then wave the knickers – exhibit one, eh? – at the judge while he's *summing up*. And they don't call out "How's that for size? I bet you couldn't get into those."'

'Sad. Very sad. Poor old Eustace. Eccentric.'

'He'd make a good Lord Chancellor.'

'But Prime Minister, we don't need one.'

'At the moment.' The Prime Minister paused to make sure his meaning had sunk in. 'So get on with it, Oswald, and make that judge shut his mouth. I don't care what you do – within limits. Why not promote him to the Court of Appeal?'

Lord Trotter gaped. 'Promote Slingsby?'

'Do a deal. Get it in writing, though. I want half-a-dozen witnesses, including a bishop. They always look good.'

'But suppose, Prime Minister, Slingsby won't play?'

'Oswald, are you out of your mind? What judge *ever* refused promotion?'

Lord Trotter, however, knew his opponent too well. 'Quite so, PM, but Slingsby is a very peculiar man.'

'He's difficult and a menace and he has to be dealt with, but he does seem to have a certain crude honesty. Why on earth did you make him a judge, Oswald?'

Trotter quickly disclaimed responsibility. 'It wasn't me, it was the Labour lot.'

Harry Minnor snorted. 'I should have known. The honest ones are always the most dangerous. It's the same with politicians. Give me a normal man every time, Oswald. You know where you are with them, you can do a deal ... Well, you see where we are now. In a hell of a bloody muddle. Your job on the line – and the whole government's position, including mine. It *has* to be ended.' The Lord Chancellor couldn't agree with him more. The question was, how?

But the Prime Minister hadn't finished yet.

'Incidentally, that Candle chap. You *can* justify putting him on the bench?'

'Judge Alwyne Chandelle-Sweet? Oh yes, absolutely. He may not set the Thames on fire, but he's very sound.' By now, Lord Trotter had said this so often that he almost believed it himself.

'And these hints about you and his wife . . ?'

'But she's my secretary, Prime Minister.'

Harry Minnor laughed. 'That doesn't give you the right to knock her off.'

'Prime Minister!' Trot gave a good impression of being deeply shocked.

'Language too crude for you, Oswald? It isn't only me that's saying it. The *Courier*, the *Sun*. You can read between the lines. But if you give me your word . . . Not that I mind about the thing itself; everybody's at it these days.'

Trot breathed a sigh of relief, as silently as he could.

'There have even been rumours about *me*.'

More than rumours, thought the Lord Chancellor, but he wisely kept his mouth shut.

'The iniquity isn't in the deed, but in the publicity, Oswald.' Now the PM sounded as if he was rehearsing a speech, and Trot sensed that the heat was being turned off.

'What a very profound remark, if I may say so, Prime Minister.'

'Then we are agreed. Good.' The Prime Minister put on his spectacles and started leafing through some papers on his desk. The interview was over.

Lord Trotter still wasn't at all sure what they were agreed about, but he thought it wise to leave it at that. It was time to consult his private secretary again – he just hoped that by now Sir Anthony had come up with something that would get Slingsby off his back for good.

3

ERIC WICKSTEAD-HACKING rang the bell to TV presenter Janet Yorke's shabby second-floor flat in a large Victorian house situated in a run-down suburb of Barfield. Fifty-nine and separated from his third wife, Eric was the barrister on the North Midland Circuit whose name was best known to the public. His cases, and the outrageous things he said while conducting them, were often reported by the local media.

Everyone knew him as Billy. At prep-school he had been called Billy Bunter on account of his flab. He never slimmed down and the name, Billy, stuck. He was a 'must' at every lawyers' party and a renowned after-dinner speaker, mainly because you never knew what he would say next. Billy himself rarely knew either, and he could be very droll when on form.

Billy was not a high-flier in court. In fact he flew so close to the ground as to be in constant danger of coming into terminal contact with it. His legal knowledge was limited, but he had a way with words, as he did with women, in spite of his unprepossessing appearance. He could amuse jurors in court, and ladies anywhere – especially in bedrooms, his favourite places, though pubs and clubs ran them close.

He had first met Janet two years ago when she interviewed him for a short spot on Channel 6 news after one of his cases hit the headlines. Billy was attracted immediately by her dark, intense good looks, and he was never one to waste time when he came across a woman he fancied. The moment the interview was finished he invited Janet to join him for a drink in a Barfield wine bar and, being at a loose end that evening, she agreed.

Janet was never quite sure afterwards how a couple of bottles of cheap Italian white wine and a bit of pâté and toast had led so quickly to coffee in her flat, then into her bed. She only knew that she had no steady man in her life at the time, was feeling low because of it, and that Billy had made her laugh and flattered her outrageously until the fact that he was definitely getting on a bit and not her type physically hadn't seemed to matter at all. The sex had been surprisingly good too, and that was a major point in Billy's favour.

After this, the two of them started seeing each other regularly, and for a while Janet persuaded herself that her relationship with Billy could turn out to be something special. But as time went by, she began to realise that Billy was not the kind of man on whom you built your hopes for the future. She also began to suspect that she was not the only woman in his life. Still, she could not help liking him and enjoying his company, and from the professional point of view his information on what was going on in local legal circles, biased though it sometimes was, often came in very useful.

Billy's practice at the Bar was entirely in crime and always for the defence. At parties Billy told people he refused to prosecute, as he did not think it ethical. He never explained what that meant, as he was not altogether sure, but it always impressed his fellow guests after a drink or two. In truth, the clerks in the Crown Prosecution Service knew that to entrust Billy with the simplest prosecution brief would invite dismissal for neglect of duty or even questions to the Attorney-General in the House of Commons.

In sum, Billy was an amusing buffoon. His lack of legal knowledge was no hindrance to him as a defending advocate, where you needed to be a ham actor rather than a profound lawyer. You only had to impress jurors, who were lay people and easily dazzled by showmanship. Judges were different and they treated Billy with sceptical disdain. He saw himself as Sir Edward Marshall Hall QC, the flamboyant defender who at the beginning of the century filled the newspapers with accounts of his famous cases. Wiser folk saw Billy as a Benny Hill or the fat one of the Two Ronnies: good company and very amusing, but not someone to whom a person with any common sense would entrust their case. One of Billy Wickstead-Hacking's problems – and this was not of his own making – was manic-depression. This strange inherited condition is suffered by about

1.4 per cent of the population: most of them intelligent and artistic, as Billy would console himself. The symptoms of the condition, which he shared with many well-known creative artists, were alternating bouts of mania and depression. In the manic phase there was a feeling of euphoria, optimism, a flight of ideas, imagination, creativity; grandiose schemes were worked on and large sums spent on impossible projects. Then came the other mood, depression, in which all was black and the subject might not even want to get out of bed. Billy's skill as an advocate and acceptability as a companion depended on which phase he happened to be in, something that he had no control over. It made life difficult at times.

Billy could trace his forebears back to 1742 when Isaac Wickstead, a shipwright turned slave-runner, married Elizabeth Mary Hacking, the daughter of a genteel but impoverished landowner who had lost most of his money in the South Sea Bubble, a swindle organised by eighteenth-century equivalents to Robert Maxwell. Isaac Wickstead almost certainly had the manic-depressive gene, and had little to give to his wife beyond Wickstead Manor near Barfield, though he put the family a notch or two up the social scale by hyphenating their names.

One of great-great-grandfather Isaac's two sons committed suicide, as did Billy's father Edward, after the long established family firm of Wickstead Rubbers – which had its origin in a West Indian rubber plantation – had been taken over. It was bought out by Astiytas, a company that made rubber goods for the very few who did not buy Durex.

Billy inherited from his father a few hundred almost worthless shares in Astiytas, manic-depression and the notion that, coming from a long established family with a double-barrelled name, he was superior to those who could not trace their forebears and had but one surname.

As a barrister, Billy had only a single claim to originality, but it was something that had spread his fame into surrounding circuits. While defending a joiner who had attempted to sever his wife's head from her body with an axe, he had hit on an unusually effective phrase. The joiner, said Billy, was so devastated by what he had done that he 'looked at life through a window of tears'.

Billy was so impressed by his own eloquence – as, it appeared, were the jury, who reduced the joiner's guilt from attempted murder to unlawful wounding – that he used the phrase with increasing frequency from then on. Every client of his, whatever the charge, sat in the dock and heard his counsel Mr Wickstead-Hacking say that he was looking at life through a window of tears. They were all impressed, as were the juries. Judges, who had heard it a dozen times before, used to put their heads in their hands at that point and groan quietly, but Billy did not mind. He knew what judges thought about him but the jurors decided cases.

Counsel who had nothing better to do used to listen to Billy in court. He was always good value, it was better than Frankie Howerd. They would often lay bets on whether Billy would drag in his favourite phrase, but the odds shortened when it became clear that Billy was determined to bring the hallowed words into every case, whatever the facts. When defending a bank manager who had ruined his life and that of his family by mixing up the bank's money with his own, it was easy: the man did indeed look at life through a window of tears. But how could even Billy justify the phrase's use in a case of reckless driving?

On the day he called at Janet Yorke's flat, Billy had been engaged in just such a case: the Queen v Harry Gosling. The court was full of barristers, waiting to hear Billy's ingenuity tested to the full as he made his final speech to the jury. Adjusting the half-moons on his stubby little nose and pulling his torn old gown around his fat little tum, Billy drew himself up to all the height and authority he could manage. His client was an unemployed twenty-five-year-old lorry driver, Harry Gosling, who had taken a bus without permission and driven it through several housing estates after an evening visiting a wide variety of licensed premises.

'Members of the Jury,' Billy began, 'as defending counsel I am like a cab on the rank of life. I have no choice as to which customers I take on board or as to the destination which any particular customer may deem appropriate. One passenger is charged with a cruel rape in sordid circumstances – leaping out on some unsuspecting girl as she walks her innocent way home through the park after a dancing lesson. Another customer in my cab is charged with a desperate bank robbery, armed with a deadly twelve-bore shotgun, carefully and deliberately shortened by sawing off the greater part of its barrel. Yet another customer in my cab, or bus if you like, it matters not, may have to face an allegation of obtaining the life-savings of an old-age pensioner, kept under the bed, after tricking his way into her house by asserting falsely that he had come there in order to read the gas-meter, or more likely the electricity-meter.'

Mr Justice Tinkering, to whom Billy was no stranger, raised his eyes to the ceiling and closed them. Several members of the jury looked deeply puzzled, as did Harry Gosling while he lounged in the dock. The jurors who were puzzled – the rest having lost all interest in the case long ago – wondered just how many offences they were concerned with. If rape, bank robbery and obtaining by false pretences came into it, why hadn't they heard evidence about them?

Instead, they had heard details of how the bus had travelled for 89.4 metres along the off-side pavement – as measured by the police – before stopping. When asked by the puzzled driver of a passing patrol-car what the bus was doing so far from its route and on the off-side pavement, Mr Gosling was alleged to have replied 'How far am I from Newport Pagnell and am I still on the M1?' Unfortunately, as the only breathalyser equipment the police had was faulty, through economies made by the Labour-controlled police committee, Mr Gosling could only be charged with reckless driving.

Billy's defence was that the driving was not reckless at all, but was either deliberate or as a result of an honest mistake, Mr Gosling having forgotten his spectacles. This explanation was only introduced by Billy in his final speech to the jury. His client did not give evidence.

The judge would have raised this as a grossly improper tactic, but he knew how hopeless it was to raise anything with Wickstead-Hacking, who went his own sweet way just the same. Even alert jurors now felt thoroughly confused about the issues in the case, which was exactly what Billy intended them to be. So long as he obtained an acquittal, it didn't matter how he did it.

It was nearly half-past five on Friday, and the jurors' minds were wandering to thoughts of food, drink and a night out with the lads – or a lass – but Billy droned on. The judge had already said he intended to finish the case that evening, even though it would mean sitting late, as it would not be fair to keep Mr Gosling in suspense over the weekend. Mr Justice Tinkering did not think it necessary to trouble the jury with the information that he and his lady clerk, both keen cricket supporters, had tickets for Lords on the following Monday and Tuesday.

After an hour and twenty minutes of repetition and irrelevance, Billy appeared to be approaching his peroration. The waiting barristers – depleted in numbers but still numbering half a dozen – anxiously listened to see who had won and who had lost their bets. Would Billy be able to employ his famous phrase, or have to admit defeat?

'As I said when I began my address to you, members of the jury, and you will perhaps accept it from me, in cases of rape, bank robbery or what-have-you, one set of words and expressions may well be appropriate. But in the case of my client Harry Gosling, who is charged as you know, with dangerous driving . . .'

'Reckless,' interposed the judge wearily.

Billy looked puzzled. 'In what way, may I ask, is your Lordship implying that I have been reckless?'

'In every way, since you ask, Mr Wickstead-Hacking. From the very start of the case. But I was trying to drive home to you, never an easy task, that your client is not charged with dangerous driving – an offence no longer known to the law – but with *reckless* driving.'

These clever, silly buggers of civil lawyers, thought Billy. They're nit-pickers – that's all Tinkering is, a tinkering nit-picker. Out loud, he simply said, 'As your Lordship pleases,' which is what barristers always say to judges when appropriate words elude them.

'Do go on please, Mr Wickstead-Hacking,' said the judge, yawning.

'I have lost my train of thought, my Lord.'

'Then you'd better get it back on the rails. It's nearly six o'clock.'

'Your Lordship is most helpful, as always,' Billy said, with a knowing look at those jurors who seemed still to be awake before he plunged on towards the climax of his speech.

'As I was saying, members of the jury' – though he had not been – 'It is now approaching a late hour, as his lordship has so helpfully reminded me. But justice must be done and seen to be done to Harry Gosling, however late the hour and despite all the slings and arrows, and indeed mud, that may be thrown at him, or indeed at me, and from whatever quarter of this ancient courtroom in our beloved Barfield. Members of the jury, I have almost done. There is little more I have to say to you. Harry Gosling will shortly be out of my hands and into your safe and capable hands. Remember that the burden of proof is always on the prosecution and the defence have to prove nothing.' Billy paused.

'Have you finished, Mr Wickstead-Hacking?' said Judge Tinkering hopefully. 'I ask because I notice you are still on your feet. I don't know if you had noticed that yourself.'

Several jurors sniggered. Money began to change hands between the barristers. It seemed that Billy's ingenuity had at last been stretched too far. But he was not finished yet.

'One final word, members of the jury. I have no means of knowing what sentence awaits my client Harry Gosling, should you find him guilty in the teeth of the evidence. It would be improper for me to speculate, as it is entirely in his Lordship's province. But imprisonment cannot be ruled out. What then would be my client's fate? Would he be looking at life through a window of tears? And would that be appropriate, members of the jury?' Triumphant, Billy sat down.

Barristers groaned. Money changed hands back again.

The judge summed up in ten minutes. In a further five minutes the jury had acquitted Mr Gosling. They were too confused, hungry and thirsty to do anything else. And so at 7.25 p.m., Billy rang the bell to Janet Yorke's flat feeling pleased with his performance in court and anticipating an even better performance in bed. He knew he was in the 'up' phase of his condition, and intended to make full use of it before the inevitable down-turn, due about a week later. His manic-depressive cycle had always been fairly regular at three months up and three months down.

Billy usually had a group of lovers – a 'team', as he thought of them – though each lady supposed she was the only woman in his life or at least, knowing Billy's reputation, did not care to enquire about her status too deeply. At that time Billy's team was headed by an American millionairess – a blue-rinsed divorcee of fifty-six named Alice Steiner. Billy had been cultivating her for three months with some success sexually but no success financially. He was beginning to think her a mean ungrateful bitch. After all, who else would fuck her so ardently at her age?

Billy was nothing if not eclectic in his tastes and his other recent lovers had included an eighteen-year-old-girl who worked at Woolworths; the wife of an oil-rig worker who found her husband's long absences lucrative but lacking in sensual excitement; the wife of an ear, nose and throat specialist who was himself knocking off two nurses and the wife of a GP; a divorced bus-conductress; and a black lesbian social worker. It had to be admitted that he had not yet made love to the latter. He had approached her as a curio and a challenge – he'd heard black women were very passionate and if he could make out with one who was a lesbian then there would surely be no limit to his sexual empire-building. However, the challenge had so far proved too much even for Billy, and he was thinking of striking her from his list.

In his most euphoric phase Billy even thought about phoning Madonna, but he didn't know her number. He prided himself on being entirely classless and fair in his choice and use of women. He didn't care how they spoke, how disappointing their table-manners were, how much they earned or where they lived (provided he did not have to travel outside a radius of twenty miles from his ancestral home of Wickstead Manor, most of which was falling down through lack of repair, though he still managed to keep the rain and rot more or less at bay in a couple of rooms). The only question Billy asked himself was 'Is she a good screw?', and he prided himself on servicing all team members with equal regularity, preferably in their homes, as it was cheaper than taking them out and more comfortable than taking them back to Wickstead Manor.

This evening it was Janet Yorke's turn. As he stood waiting for her to open the door he wondered how much longer he could keep it up – his work with the team. He might have to reduce it by dispensing with some of the women – but that would not be easy as they all had different quirks and preferences, and it was the variety that made for enjoyment. He couldn't understand how any man could manage with one woman only; probably only the very young, the very old and the very gay did. The door opened and he was surprised to see Janet in her peach towelling dressing-gown. That was unusual, though welcome – it wasted less time.

'I thought you were coming yesterday, Billy,' said Janet reproachfully.

He hadn't had another mix-up, had he, thought Billy. He needed a secretary to sort out his appointments and prevent cock-ups like this. The trouble was he couldn't afford to pay for one and she couldn't be part of the team because she'd have to know about all the other women.

He decided to ignore his mistake and act as if nothing had happened. 'What are you doing this evening, Janet?'

'Why? Thinking of taking me out to dinner?' Janet said in a way that showed how improbable she thought the idea was. 'It's about time you did.'

'Well ... I wish I could. But I've brought you this.' Billy produced a bottle from his overcoat, like a conjurer producing a rabbit from a hat.

Janet examined it, unimpressed. 'Lambrusco, eh? We *are* lashing out. That's about as alcoholic as Lucozade.'

'But I'm driving, Janet.'

'Still got that clapped out old Volvo?'

Billy looked sheepish. He wanted to sit down

and have a drink, but Janet had made no move to invite him in. 'I'm hoping to change it soon. You can take me out in your car if you'd rather.'

'It's off the road, Billy. I can't afford to insure it.'

'I thought your TV work was doing okay!' said Billy, genuinely surprised.

Janet grimaced. 'It's fallen off since I had to go freelance.'

'I liked your TV programme with Trotter and Slingsby the other night.' Billy was now trying hard to ingratiate himself. He had in fact missed the programme, but he was anxious to get her in a good mood, or his mission would have to be aborted.

'Trotter's a bastard,' Janet said, pulling her dressing-gown more tightly round her.

'Don't expect me to agree. The only barristers who can say that about the Lord Chancellor are those who've made it on to the bench and don't want promotion, or who know they'll never get it.'

'But you know you'll never get it, Billy.'

'I've applied nine times.' Billy's tone was aggrieved. 'Nowadays all I get is a short letter from Anthony Kingston saying I'm being considered. Then you don't hear any more. They *are* bastards up there in London, you're right.'

'I expect you want to go to bed, Billy.'

He perked up. 'Sounds a good idea.'

'Well, you can't. You're a day too late. I've started.'

And I've finished, thought Billy, as she shut the door firmly in his face. Oh well, some you win and some you lose. He wondered if his bus conductress had finished her shift for the evening.

The Lord Chancellor was in urgent conclave with his permanent secretary. It was a council of war. Something *had* to be done about the unprecedented situation regarding Raymond Slingsby. Even though High Court judges were virtually unsackable, lord chancellors had kept them firmly in line for centuries. Trot had never heard of any judge, prior to Slingsby, standing up to a holder of the Great Seal.

The Lord Chancellor alone decided who to appoint to the bench and promote further up the ladder. In accordance with tradition Trot usually took soundings from existing judges, especially the Lord Chief Justice and Master of the Rolls, but he did not have to. He could appoint to the bench any qualified person that he chose. Judges were happy to accept a system that had selected them. Would-be judges dared not challenge the system, or it would not select them. Lay persons had no choice and no voice; the law dealt with them and their problems daily, but that did not qualify them for any part in the selection process.

On the whole, judges were not rebellious types, or they would not have been chosen. The judiciary was a small tight world and the judges had to get on with each other. Anyway, most judges wanted something from the Lord Chancellor and his top men, and not only promotion. There were memberships of royal commissions to be had, or the opportunity of presiding over a high-profile committee to inquire into a disaster such as that at Sheffield football ground.

Only a thoroughly eccentric man such as Raymond Slingsby would turn his back on all this. He had not only refused a knighthood, he had even had the nerve to turn down the chance of attending a Buckingham Palace garden party – something that was automatically offered to all judges when appointed to the bench. In fact he wrote an extraordinary letter to the then Lord Chancellor objecting to Palace garden parties on principle:

Dear Lord Chancellor

I have received a written request, which must have been inspired by your office, asking if my wife and I wish to be invited to a garden party at Buckingham Palace. The letter indicated that even if we were to answer in the affirmative, there was no guarantee that we would in fact receive an invitation.

I would always hesitate before accepting an 'invitation' couched in such terms. Who do the people at the Palace think they are? I know what I think they are – toffee-nosed hangers-on who should be employed in some useful work such as digging up roads or emptying dustbins, instead of organising tomfool 'royal' events.

My wife and I have no wish to put on fancy clothes for such a pointless occasion. My morning-suit no longer fits me and I do not intend to buy a replacement. And why should any sane person whose mind is not besotted with snobbish ideas wish to queue for a cup of tea and a bun in the hope of catching a glimpse of Royal Personages? Or are High Court judges on the list of those selected for personal presentation to HM? I neither know nor care and I will never know the answer or bother tuppence about it. Such distinctions are out of place today or should be. It is understandable that provincial mayors and small businessmen and their wives should wish to show off to their friends by casually letting drop that they have been to the Palace, and that is what royalty is about. It is part of the class system that hobbles the English – not so much the Welsh or Scots – and makes us look absurd in the eyes of other nations, and a reason for our slipping into Second World, approaching Third World, status.

You will not agree with me, but I ask you – what is royalty? It is nothing to do with government. Is it part of the entertainment industry? If so, I regret I do not find the activities of any of the so-called royals to be entertaining in any way that means something. If royalty is part of the export trade, we should export the lot of them to the highest bidder – presumably Japan or some state of America. Let the auction begin.

Believe me, Lord Chancellor, my wife and I are not interested, and we do not wish to make an unnecessary and socially parasitic visit to that architectural nonsense known as Buckingham Palace. No disrespect is intended to anybody.

The letter was pinned to the inside cover of Slingsby's file with the comment, 'Unbelievable!', written below in red ink by Sir Anthony Kingston.

It infuriated Lord Trotter as he re-read it. This letter alone should be justification enough for removing Raymond Slingsby from Her Majesty's bench of High Court judges. There was no place there for an outcast who thumbed his nose at our dear Queen, who did so much and worked so hard for the nation. The monarchy held the country together at the top, and if we were to lose it – unthinkable thought! – we would be like a man beheaded.

The Rt Hon. Lord Trotter of St Pancras and Sir Anthony Kingston KCB agreed, as they sipped their coffee, that what was needed was a return to the golden days of the good and great Lord Hailsham of St Marylebone. The rot had set in when this proud patrician was succeeded – after the brief interlude of Lord Havers – by Lord Chancellor Mackay, a Scot.

Lord Mackay had done a shocking thing when he abolished the Kilmuir Rules that let the Lord Chancellor decide which judges should speak to the media. No wonder everything had gone wrong under the new system: *the puppets were pulling the strings*! What the system of justice needed was a man at the top who was strong enough to dispense with justice when dealing with judges whose job was to dispense it.

'I won't have it, Kingston,' blustered Lord Trotter. 'All my efforts, everything I've worked for all my life, my public service, sacrifices. I'm not going to see it all blown away because of this jumped-up jumble of a judge from the North. If he makes that speech next week, if we let him, that will be the end for all of us.'

Sir Anthony smiled a thin-lipped smile. Unlike his master, he had actually been doing some constructive thinking since their last meeting. 'Worry not, sir, I think I have the solution. Eric Wickstead-Hacking.'

Lord Trotter was unimpressed. 'Who the devil's he?'

'He's a barrister on the North Midland who used to be in chambers with Slingsby at Barfield. Everyone calls him Billy, by the way. He knows the judge well but doesn't like his politics. I've sounded him out – through a third party, of course – and he says he'll help.'

'How much does he want?' Lord Trotter had not lost his pragmatic approach.

'Money doesn't come into it,' said Sir Anthony primly.

'You mean, he runs a charity for this sort of thing?'

'Your Lordship has ample patronage at your disposal,' the permanent secretary pointed out.

Lord Trotter sighed. 'I suppose you're suggesting that I should make *him* a Circuit judge?'

'He's very anxious to be one. In fact he's already applied, several times, but I turned him down.'

The Lord Chancellor sighed again. Then he asked to see Billy's file and flicked through it, remarking that it didn't look any better than Chandelle-Sweet's record. And if he went on appointing Circuit judges like *him*, the Circuit bench would be full of half-wits – as some people thought it was already.

Lord Trotter then learned that his permanent secretary, in an astonishing show of initiative, had already arranged for Billy to come and see them in two days' time at 10.30 a.m. Trot realised that he had been backed into a corner. He would have to play it by ear, having only a vague notion of what the tune would be, but desperate times called for desperate remedies. Maybe this man Billy Wickstead-Hacking would have some miraculous answer to the Slingsby problem. Maybe everything would turn out all right, in the end. But another part of Trot murmured to himself 'Maybe ... and maybe we're only getting ourselves deeper and deeper in the shit.'

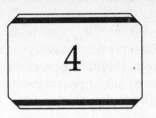

4

'GOT HIM!' said Mr Justice Slingsby.
    'Who?'
'Both of them.'

Ray and his wife were sitting up in their twin beds at the Lodgings. Both of them were reading – he the *Courier*, which had just been delivered, and she the *Kennel*, the monthly organ of the Royal Society for the Protection of Dogs, which she had been devouring daily since its arrival a week earlier.

'What is it now, dear?' Helen was only half-concentrating on Ray's explosive remark. *Kennel* had reported her appointment as national chairman of the RSPD and she had been re-reading the announcement, which gave her great pride.

'Judge Sweet.' Ray thought it as unnecessary to pronounce the Chandelle as it was for the so-called judge to include it in his ridiculous surname.

'What about him?' Helen still only had one ear available for her husband.

'The *Courier* have been digging up the dirt on him.'

'How very unfair, Ray. And how typical of them.'

Ray quoted from the paper with relish: 'Judge Chandelle-Sweet has always claimed he graduated from Sheffield university with second-class honours in law, a necessary qualification for becoming a barrister. But the *Courier* has discovered he is a liar. He only went to that university for one year and did not even sit the examination at the end of it. They never saw him again. In his application form at the Council of Legal Education there are forged details.'

Ray stopped reading. 'It's bad for Sweet, and worse for Trot.'

'But dear,' protested Helen, determined to be fair, 'would the Lord Chancellor know about the degree – that there wasn't one?'

'It doesn't matter. At the very least it shows what a rotten system they have for selecting judges.'

'It selected you, dear.'

Ray felt cross. Helen wasn't applying her mind to the question. What did the selection of judges matter to her, so long as all those wretched dogs were properly fed and weren't ill-treated? Animals meant more to her than people, these days.

'What's going to happen now, Ray?'

Helen still hadn't raised her eyes from that ridiculous magazine. What an absurd nation the British were – dog-mad, he thought.

'There will be questions in Parliament about Sweet.'

'There always are, but who takes any notice?' murmured Helen.

'You would, if somebody asked the Minister about the ill-treatment of some obscure mongrel.' His voice was bitter.

'Ray, that isn't fair,' said Helen, sitting up and taking notice at last. 'I know you feel strongly about the Chandelle-Sweet business, but it'll be over and done with soon.'

'It'll be swept under the carpet, you mean. Things usually are, Helen. That's what's wrong with this damnable country of ours.'

'You mustn't get things out of proportion, Ray.' Helen turned back to *Kennel*.

What an infuriating woman. Would she never show concern for anything except those wretched animals? He and Helen were not on the same wavelength, never had been and never would be. He had known it for years but had never spoken of it. It wasn't either's fault that they were as they were, but marriage should be a unity of mind and body, and they were at one in neither.

All passion spent. There had been some at the beginning on his part though very little on hers, ever: not active passion, but passive compliance. Anyway such rapture as there had ever been had long since evaporated. Maybe it did with every marriage.

If only things had gone right with the German girl. He should have handled it better; he'd been far too eager and frightened her off. It would

83

never have happened if he'd had more experience. Ray had always longed for a full relationship, an all-systems-go relationship, functioning flat out at every level – but could it exist, in real life? Maybe such things happened only in films, but it didn't stop people like him dreaming about them. Even though he would never do anything about it and would gradually sink into the dust accepting what he did not find acceptable, compromising and fudging as most people did all their lives.

He lay there and pondered. Then he looked across at Helen who had nodded off – that just about summed it up and maybe that's what he should do, nod off and forget about the Lord Chancellor and how rotten he was, and how rotten the system was that Trot presided over and wanted to perpetuate.

Some people said that Ray got too worked up about things, and he should pipe down and enjoy life. But he wasn't made like that, and he hadn't felt like that ever. He had always said what he thought and fought for what he thought was right, and be damned to the consequences. He wasn't going to back down, but would press on till Trotter and all he symbolised were exposed and, he hoped, replaced by something better, if that could be achieved in this slumbering land.

In any case, what had he to lose? He couldn't be sacked, except in theory by Parliament, and that never happened. He would not get promotion to the Court of Appeal, certainly not under Trot, but what did that matter? He had never been all that ambitious even to be a judge, and maybe he was wrong to accept it when the Labour Lord Chancellor pressed it on him, there being no other suitable socialist candidate for the High Court bench.

All right then, Ray concluded, in this battle within himself. It was war to the death – him or Trot. Any chance he got to carry the fight to Lord Trotter, through the Alwyne Sweet thing, or any other weapon that came to hand, he'd go ahead whatever it cost him. He would pull no punches to the magistrates at Chesterfield next week. He was going to let Trotter and his rotten appointments system have it with both barrels. Be damned to Trotter, Sweet and the rest of that complacent, stuck-up lot. The time had come for him to speak out, in plain defiant language. Ray jumped out of bed and went briskly to the bathroom where, bracing himself, he had an ice-cold shower.

No-Knickers had spent the whole night with her employer, something she rarely dared to do and did not enjoy anyway. Trot had insisted, though, and now that it was morning he was trying in vain to make it with her again. She was becoming more and more disgusted with him, and frustrated too. Fucking was what their relationship had been about, and now he could hardly manage that with any hardness or endurance, what was left?

Yesterday evening when he fed his manhood into her, it soon slipped out, about as rigid as a semi-frozen piece of rope. Enough was enough, thought No-Knickers – or rather it wasn't nearly enough. She felt trapped. Her husband had neither the ability nor the will for it; her toy-boy was not available. In Glasgow on business, he said, though as he had never had any employment of any kind other than as a stud, she wondered if the explanation was wholly true.

And now, piston-like Trot could piston no longer. His big-end had gone – wasn't that what car men said? Even after charging his batteries overnight, which he predicted would sort things out, it had been no better, no firmer. He had things on his mind, as the whole nation knew, but No-Knickers could feel little sympathy for him even as he lay on top of her, grunting and sweating.

'Can't concentrate today. Try again later.' The Lord Chancellor rolled his bulk off his private secretary.

'Don't worry, Trot, it'll come back,' though she was beginning to hope it wouldn't. 'You've got too much to worry about, that's the trouble.'

'Yes,' said the Lord Chancellor, whose temper had not been improved by his failure. 'The continuing fiasco of your husband.'

'Did you know about the Sheffield university thing when you made him a judge?'

'Of course not,' snapped Trot. 'Did you?'

'I always assumed he had a degree – he certainly never told me he didn't. But shouldn't you have checked – asked to see a certificate or something?'

'Nonie, when a barrister says he is one, you don't query it. The same with a degree.'

Anona persisted,'Shouldn't Kingston have checked?'

'Well, to be absolutely truthful,' said Trot reluctantly, knowing that his private secretary was one of the few people who had access to the papers in question, 'we had heard rumours that there was something fishy about your Alwyne and his time at Sheffield. There's a reference on the file. But we didn't pay any attention to it.'

Anona stifled a desire to laugh. 'You made a balls of it, didn't you? And Slingsby will have you by the balls, if that note on the file comes out.'

'It won't. It will be mislaid. In any case, Nonie, there's no need for pessimism. Help is at hand: our saviour will be here at half-past ten tomorrow morning.'

Anona knew Trot no longer believed in the second coming, religious or sexual, so she assumed this must be a real person.

'A barrister called Wickstead-Hacking,' Trot went on.

Anona sat bolt upright in bed. 'Not Billy! They say he's the craziest barrister who's never been actually certified. What on earth's he going to do for you?'

'Help us out with Slingsby,' said Trot vaguely. He still didn't actually know what Kingston and Wickstead-Hacking had in mind.

'And what's he hoping to get out of it?'

'Well, if he's successful, he may possibly be considered . . .'

Fucking hell, thought Nonie, not another Circuit judge. 'It's time I got out of here,' she said out loud.

'Out of bed?'

87

'The Lord Chancellor's office. It's becoming a madhouse.'

That upset Lord Chancellor Trotter, but worse, it worried him. What if Nonie went and blabbed to the *Courier* or the *Sun*? They'd pay thousands for her story. Should he get this Wickstead-Hacking to shut her mouth at the same time as Slingsby's?

If Nonie meant what she said, she would have to be dealt with. Not killed – even for Trotter that would be going too far, besides it could give the office of the Lord Chancellor a bad name. Emasculation – that's what Slingsby deserved. But in Nonie's case – what was the word? Perhaps there wasn't one for women. De-feminized? That was happening to her already. She was getting too fat. Those mellowing melons that had once been such forbidden and enticing fruit were going off, and the taste was beginning to repel him. Everything was falling apart. It all rested on Wickstead-Hacking now, and he had better deliver. If he did, nothing would be too good for the man. Well, perhaps not a High Court judgeship. There were limits, even to the Lord Chancellor's desperation.

Trot and Anona lay in bed naked, eyeing each other like two seals in the rutting season. Then there was an ugly sound: a key was turning in the door to the flat. Only Kingston had a key, in the safe in an envelope marked 'For use in case of fire only'. The door opened and footsteps approached.

'Kingston, is that you?' called Trot.

There was no reply but the footsteps came nearer. The bedroom door was flung open, and

Trot froze, incapable of speech or action. Nonie screamed and rammed her head under the bedclothes as though she'd seen a ghost. Massive Lady Emeline Trotter stood framed in the doorway in a menacing pose. Holding a horsewhip as if she was about to use it, she marched forward. Then with one sweep of her brawny arm she removed the bed-clothes which partially concealed the two bodies.

On weekday mornings, His Honour Judge Alwyne Chandelle-Sweet usually left his Wimbledon semi after his wife. While Nonie had to leave at seven in order to perform confidential services for her employer Lord Trotter, Alwyne never sat in court before ten-thirty – it wasn't fair to those who had to travel to court from a distance, he said.

This morning, however, his wife was not there. Nonie had told Alwyne she had an urgent mission for her employer in Leicester. It was so hush-hush she was forbidden to mention it to anyone except her husband, and even he could not be told where she was staying, or be given the phone number.

As it turned out, it was fortunate for No-Knickers that she was absent. Throughout the night the house had been surrounded by a brigade of media people. They came and went in relays, camping on the lawn and coming up to bang on the door from time to time in a vain attempt to get a response from Judge Chandelle-Sweet.

'A statement, your Honour. That's all we want, a statement and then we'll go away,' they shouted.

Poor Alwyne spent a wretched night prowling the house in his pyjamas and dressing-gown, shrinking from the windows as he went from room to room trying to see what was happening outside without being seen.

Whenever the reporters caught a glimpse of him, the Circuit judge was flashed at by several dozen cameras. 'Sir, sir. Stand there, please, sir. Do you mind opening the window please? Sir, sir,' shouted their operators.

'Come outside,' shouted the *Daily Express* reporter, who had been brought by the sisterly *Star* lady. He was off the road for the third time for accepting one drink too many and the two of them, both married to others, were having a searing affair.

'We would like a discreet word with you, your Honour,' called the *Guardian* lady in a deep, educated voice, but she could barely be heard by anyone, especially as she was standing next to the almost legless lout from the *Courier*. His main contribution to the cacophony was to yell, 'Come out, you fucking arsehole of a judge,' to which – even if he heard it – the judge unsurprisingly made no response.

The young man from the *Sun* showed himself the most practical of the press persons present. He took a ladder from the next-door-neighbour's yard, placed it at the back of the judicial residence and climbed up it. There was no window open, so he had to force himself over the gutter and on to the roof, hoping to enter through a skylight.

Meanwhile the lout from the *Courier*, ever eager

to see the *Sun* go down, was not too legless to remove the ladder. The *Sun* man was left isolated on the roof, unsuccessfully trying to hide behind the chimney stack. He knew all too well that if his rival papers' photographers should snap him up there, their editors would gleefully picture him on their front page the following morning. Several did just that, causing the *Sun* man to have a painful interview with his editor, who was said to have been less than his usual quiet, urbane and courteous self.

In difficult situations, Alwyne usually consulted his wife Anona, who after all had the highest lawyer in the land above her. How very sad then that now, when he needed her most, she was holed up in some anonymous Leicester hotel performing her dedicated duty to Lord Trotter. So Alwyne had to make a decision alone, aided only by such insight and common sense as he possessed. Unhappily, though not for the first time in his life, he made the wrong one.

He stepped outside, holding up both hands. Cameras clicked, tape-recorders recorded and video cameras silently compiled a record of the moving scene for all time. In holding both arms skyward, and indeed *Sun*-ward, his Honour Judge Alwyne Chandelle-Sweet intended to silence the multitude, which was being added to every minute. (*Le Figaro* and *Paris Match* had come, and even *Pravda* had by this time joined in, determined to record a typical savaging of the Establishment by itself. That, at least, is what the *Pravda* lady wrote. She had been trained at the Soviet Press

School and even after the New Revolution had been unable to reorientate herself.)

The arms-raised pictures were variously interpreted by the world's press. None gave the true interpretation, of course. The *Sun* splashed JUDGE GIVES IN. Showing a surprising variation the *Courier* version was JUDGE GIVES UP. The *Star* told the world in a moment of spontaneity that kept Fleet Street bars giggling for months, NO-DEGREE JUDGE PLEADS: NO THIRD DEGREE. The *Guardian* had six lines at the foot of a column towards the back of the paper. The first and last lines had been transposed but this made little difference to the way it read for those few readers who had persevered to page twenty-two.

When he left the shelter of his front door, Alwyne was instantly surrounded. Tape-recorders and cameras were thrust at him while questions were fired like Chinese crackers. The reporters all asked the same questions. 'What about the degree?' 'Are you a fraud?' 'Are you for the chop?' 'What does Lord Trotter say and where's No-Knickers?' If all had spoken in unison the words would have been clear, but showing an independence and lack of conformity that in other circumstances would have been commendable, each questioner put the phrases in a different sequence. This made it very difficult to understand what any of them were saying.

The scrum moved slowly towards the conservatory at the side of the house, with everyone shoving and pulling and shouting.

'Please, please, gentlemen. Please, gentlemen,' Alwyne kept calling.

The women media people noted this sexual discrimination and used it in their pieces, the *Guardian* person especially – was not the Womens' Page the central feature of that great organ?

When the scrum arrived at the conservatory, logically it should have stopped, but the uncontrolled mob of journalists had thrown logic to the winds. So they all continued as if no-one had seen the obstacle, and the smashing and splintering of glass added to the cacophony.

'Look what you've done. You've widened the door,' cried his Honour, almost in tears. By this time some order had at last instilled itself into the press corps.

'A statement. Give us a statement,' they called in unison. As shards of the conservatory – which with its roof now open to the sky more closely resembled an observatory – fell in a Christmassy crystallised tinkle, Alwyne again held up both arms. 'That's it, sir. Hold it. Once again please, sir,' chorused the photographers. There was a tinkling hush.

'Gentlemen of the press,' Alwyne began. The *Guardian* lady let out a shriek and dropped her tape-recorder. 'Gentlemen, I implore you. Please, look what you've done.'

'We want to know what *you've* done,' called the man from *The Times*. He had just been transferred from the *Courier* and wanted to convince his colleagues that, despite his provenance, he was not only intelligent but witty with it.

Alwyne tried again. 'Sit down, gentlemen, please.'

But they all preferred to stand, as the chairs were covered by menacing pieces of glass. The reporters wanted to get to the bottom of things but there were limits. Questions were now shot at his Honour as if from competing automatic weapons. Lacking any other means of selection, the judge chose to answer those that were shouted most loudly and repeatedly.

'Have you, or have you not a law degree from Sheffield university?'

'I thought I had, but I haven't been able to find it.'

This was a shrewder reply than Alwyne himself realised. Even the press people were confused.

'What do you mean, you can't find it?'

'Where did you lose it?'

'Did you get one or didn't you?'

'How could you get a degree after one year?'

Then the *Courier* representative, who had been up and about since five a.m. and kept trying to revive himself with liquid from an unmarked container, fired off what he thought was a corker: 'Judge, are you a complete arsehole or are you not?'

He was shouting this more loudly and more frequently than any other question, so Alwyne, anxious to be fair and consistent, tried to think of an appropriate response. He found it hard. Should he deny he was a complete arsehole, thereby implying that he was an incomplete one? Should he try to be rational in a judge-like way and 'confess and avoid' – admit that he had an arsehole but deny that the word applied to him in a wider context?

His Honour Judge Alwyne Chandelle-Sweet solved the dilemma in a brave British manner by avoiding it. He made a sudden dash through the unprepared and by now bleary-eyed gathering, sprinting across the garden and into the road still wearing his pyjamas and dressing-gown.

The press people pursued him at varying speeds, young Alec from the *Sunday Sport* leading the field. He steadied and readied his camera as he ran. His newspaper was economising on staff and did not feel able to justify the use of two people if one could both scribble and click. Alec had shown little interest in the proceedings so far, but seeing the judicial dressing-gown opening and the judicial pyjamas descending as his Honour fled, he realised his duty to his readers.

Police Sergeant Tom Spudding stood in the road by his police car. He had so far hesitated to intervene. This was partially because that was his usual style – the hands-off approach to situations of conflict. 'I won't get involved unless I have to,' he used to tell new recruits. Things had a way of sorting themselves out if you left them alone. Suspects ran off and potential witnesses went home, destroying any possibility of tiresome legal proceedings.

Sergeant Spudding found preparing statements tedious and as for giving evidence, he hated it – those clever lawyers only wanted to make fools out of people like him. So he never went looking for trouble, and when on surveillance duties took an attitude that was relaxed – so relaxed at times that he nodded off. That had happened this morning. It was only when he heard the mob thundering and shrieking towards him that he emerged from his patrol car, rubbing his eyes.

What should he do? It was a long time since he studied *Moriarty's Police Law* and he only had seventeen months, two weeks and three days to go to retirement. No point in risking unnecessary conflict or even – perish the thought – bruises, at this stage, thought the sergeant. He was still debating whether or not to assert himself, when the trouble asserted itself, arriving in the shape of his Honour Judge Alwyne Chandelle-Sweet. Sergeant Spudding failed to recognise the judge. That was understandable. He had only seen him in public and fully dressed. Now the judge was partly undressed and showing parts of himself that could only be termed private. Indecent exposure, thought the sergeant. Shall I do this chap for it, he wondered, stepping forward. He was still wondering when Alwyne ran slap bang into him, and both men fell to the ground, the sergeant flat on his back and the judge on top of him, arse fully exposed.

No body of journalists has ever scribbled and recorded so avidly, no photographers clicked with such repeated fervour. The tabloids and their picture-editors thought it must be Christmas. There was so much in this astonishing story to choose from, where should they begin? Splash headlines had to be un-splashed and re-splashed, whole front pages 'pulled' and replaced. The unions would never have stood for it in the old days.

JUDGE LAYS ON THE LAW was the *Sun*'s not wholly grammatical contribution. There was a large picture showing the judge's bottom, the sergeant's stripes on Tom Spudding's tunic and the look of surprise on his face. An arrow pointed to the exposed rear end, so that the readers at the bottom end of the market would not be confused.

The *Mirror* had BOTTOMS UP – JUDGE EXPOSED. The editor of the *Star* was not at his brilliant best when he penned JUDGE COPS SERGEANT, and the *Courier* was thought by Fleet Street to have won the battle of the splashes with WHOOPS!. What could beat that, in a tabloid industry devoted to sentences as short as possible and words that were not only brief but telling?

Apart from Alwyne himself, the person most devastated by all this was Prime Minister Harry Minnor. The following morning, he sat in his study at No. 10 with the newspapers set out before him like huge black playing cards in a game being played with the devil, who was represented on earth – he was now convinced – by Lord Chancellor Trot, bloody effing Trotter. The PM thought that his Lord Chancellor had brought the state of the law as low as could be. His bewildering appointment of this appalling barefaced, now bare-arsed, judge could no longer be overlooked.

Harry's eyes squeezed out tiny tears – not of grief but of uncontrollable frustration. His hand hovered towards the phone on his desk and then withdrew several times. He could not make up his mind whether to sack Trotter there and then. On the face of it that looked like the best way of defusing the situation, but would it? The tabloids might simply go from one humiliating splash to another and the whole affair would never end until the whole government had been dragged down into oblivion.

What was the answer? End it all now, for ever? Harry had a rusty old revolver in his desk, a gift from the Iraqi ambassador, the significance of which he had never been able to determine. But did it fire? Would British ammunition fit, and would it do to send the Special Branch on a purchasing mission? If they asked why, he couldn't very well say 'Because I want to shoot myself.' They might refuse to go, report him to the Queen – the only person above him. Or was there God too?

He must pull himself together, keep cool, as he did after he'd landed the jumbo without the benefit of wheels. Agonising though the moment was, he had remembered to blame the equipment and deny any fault of his own. The PM took a deep breath, lifted the phone and dialled the Lord Chancellor's private number.

Billy Wickstead-Hacking drove south down the M1. At least he hoped it was south, though he remembered the time when he had driven twenty-six miles along the M6 in the wrong direction, having muddled up Preston and Birmingham –

the sort of mistake that could happen to anybody. But on this balmy morning, barmy Billy – as he was intelligent enough to know some of his colleagues at the Bar thought him – was in a very good mood. This was not attributable only to the present euphoric phase in his cycle. Billy was convinced that the moment he had awaited for so long had come. He had almost given up hope of elevation to the Circuit bench, but for what other conceivable reason had Lord Trotter himself sent for him? Not to discuss the weather or the state of the stock market. It must be in answer to his repeated applications, made year after year in carefully worded documents, to be considered for appointment as one of Her Majesty's Circuit judges.

Billy pressed harder on the accelerator of his Volvo 240 estate, with its cherished number BLY 98. Volvos changed so little year by year, and the number was the easiest and cheapest way of hiding the age of his antique vehicle. BLY was the nearest he could get to BILLY and 98 was the nearest available number to one that he could afford. The car did not respond to the coaxing, or indeed to the violent pressure, of Billy's right foot.

It had been a faithful vehicle, this stoutly built Volvo, but age takes its toll on all of us, thought Billy sadly. He quickly moved his right foot to the centre pedal in order to avoid collision with a clapped-out S-registered lorry, whose driver had thoughtlessly applied his brakes without warning. Billy cursed as he avoided the lorry by inches, as he had avoided so many dangerous-looking encounters throughout his interesting life.

There had been hard times – especially in 'down' periods, which one had to accept and grit one's way through – but the good times, the 'highs' had been really good and now the best time of all was coming. At fifty-nine, when he had all but abandoned hope, his ship – or his Volvo – was coming into port or carport or whatever. Make way for his Honour Judge Eric Wickstead-Hacking. He had had enough of 'Billy'. The name had a familiar and friendly ring, but dignity would be called for on the bench. Anyone who called him Billy after his swearing-in ceremony would receive a coolly deliberate cold shoulder. Even the Lord Chancellor himself, should he chance to employ the nickname, would receive the same treatment. After he'd sworn Billy in, of course, not before.

A new Volvo, that's what he would buy, once empanelled on the bench, thought Billy. He had been looking forward to a brand new one. This one had done – he glanced at the mileometer – 212,898 miles. Even Volvos did not last for ever, though it was claimed that most of those that had ever been made were still alive. But now: would it be a 940 or an 850GLT? By the time he had made up his mind, Billy was only about sixty miles from London. Yes, it would be the revolutionary (for Volvo) front-wheel drive Volvo 850GLT. He only hoped his current model, in spite of its slipping clutch, would emulate his own determination to get to the great man by ten-thirty next morning. 'Looking at life through a window of tears': that had been his own situation for more years than he cared to recall. He remembered the time he was black-balled by the Garrick Club – founded in seventeen hundred and something and still a haunt of actors and lawyers. Billy thought the black-baller might have been Mr Justice Tinkering. On the other hand, Lord Chief Justice Black could have done it because of Billy's part in the case of the Inebriated Pigeon, which he heard in the Court of Appeal (Criminal Division).

Billy had been instructed in that case by little Harry Loddy, a middle-aged solicitor member of an old – indeed geriatric – Barfield family. Harry had sent the brief in the pigeon case to Billy because no other counsel was available. The lay client – the defendant to a charge of house-burglary – was Steven Cocking, aged sixty-two. He had been found by PC Donald Bloodworthy in the house in question at 3.20 a.m., having broken a pane of glass in the back door while wearing gloves. Apart from the glass, nothing had been taken or disturbed.

PC Bloodworthy received a public commendation from the judge for arriving on the scene so quickly, but when the judge asked for the source of his information the officer said such details could not be revealed or they would prejudice informants. In fact, he had simply been passing the house and knowing the occupants, friends of his, were in Tenerife until the following Saturday, he had thought the sight of a man moving around upstairs with a torch merited investigation.

One of the duties of a solicitor with a practice in crime is to 'assist' a client with his 'proof of evidence', which accompanies the brief to counsel. Harry probed the defendant's story at Barfield prison, where the defendant was in custody despite weekly applications for bail – he had fifty-nine convictions for house-burglary on his record, in addition to an enterprising assortment of other crimes. Harry showed excitement when his client happened to mention he was a pigeon-fancier. That could be the key.

'Suppose,' he said to Steve, 'Just suppose – and I am not allowed to suggest anything to you; that would be quite wrong and against the rules. But suppose one of your pigeons happened to escape, and you went looking for it and saw it in the house during the night, it having gone down the chimney. What would you do?'

Steve, who was not a Sumo champion when it came to seizing the point, replied, 'But one of my pigeons didn't escape.'

Harry tried again. 'I was only saying, suppose it did.'

'But it didn't,' Steve persisted stubbornly. 'And anyway,' he went on, 'why would it go down that chimney? My pigeons would never do that, not one of them. I've trained them all – since I got out after my last bit of bad luck. I know them all by name.'

Harry was not to be put off. 'Aah, but if one of them got drunk, he might do anything – he could *fall* down the chimney.'

Steve gawped at him. 'But pigeons don't drink – not beer and stuff like that.'

Was there no end to the man's stupidity? How could Harry maintain a flourishing practice with such dim clients? The solicitor's invention soared like the imaginary pigeon.

'The pigeon could have been accidentally locked in a room in your house . . .'

'My pigeons have their own loft.'

'Yes, but if it was sick, you could have brought it into the house to recuperate.'

Steve wasn't sure what recuperate meant, but had a vague idea. 'Yeah, it could happen. But it never has, mind.'

At last, felt Harry, he was getting the case on its feet.

'But look,' Steve said, 'Isn't it better if I plead guilty? I mean, it were a fair cop.'

'I don't think he was fair at all; he entirely misunderstood your reason for being in that house. And as for pleading guilty, you're not doing yourself justice, you know, so how can you expect justice at Barfield Crown Court?' Harry thought it unnecessary to explain that at that time a defending solicitor was paid by the hour, and earned much more on a contested case than a guilty plea.

'But the pigeon would have been there. And where did it get its beer, anyway?'

'That's easy: you could have left a glass partly finished when you went to bed. Pigeon is thirsty – you've forgotten to leave it some water. It goes for the only available liquid, drinks too much, isn't used to it, feels like a flutter outside, notices an open window and whoosh. Bob's your uncle.'

This flight of fancy impressed Steve. He smiled slowly. 'Oh, I see. It could all have happened, I suppose, if you put it like that.'

All this was carefully typed into the brief marked 'R v Steven Cocking. Mr Eric Wickstead-Hacking. Legal Aid', tied with red ribbon, and sent to counsel's clerk. Billy read it with interest tinged with a degree of scepticism. He knew Harry Loddy, and thought that short-story writing would have been a more appropriate career for him than the law. But it wasn't for him to query his instructions; it was his duty to accept them and act on them.

The Crown Court trial was before assistant recorder Gordon Heathersedge, a solicitor sitting at the Crown Court for only the second occasion and very anxious not to blot his record and thus imperil his ambition to become a Circuit judge. Accordingly he did his very best to try the case fairly.

The case went much better for the defence than Harry Loddy and Billy had anticipated. Steve was dressed in his best suit, clean-shaven and with his hair done neatly. In the witness-box he described himself as a 'company director' and there was some substance in that. A year or so previously Harry Loddy had thought it prudent to assist Steve – a good and regular client – by making him the director of a shell company, Barfield Plastics, which had an accommodation address but no assets, premises or employees, had never traded and never would.

The Crown Prosecution Service and the police were so overwhelmed with work that they neglected to discover those facts, so Steve was not questioned about them when in the box. Even so, the jury – which happened to have on it a retired police superintendent from another force – said 'guilty' by ten-two and the sentence was nine months.

Assistant recorder Heathersedge knew the usual 'tariff' was eighteen months but thought it unnecessary to encourage an appeal and invite the real possibility that the Court of Appeal (Criminal Division) might contain three of its more lenient members with no experience, at the Bar or in life, of criminals.

However, there *was* an appeal against conviction, after Harry and Billy had held a three-hour conference, paid for by the hour. The grounds of the appeal ran to four closely typed pages and had one arguable point: the assistant recorder had erred when directing the jury that there was no evidence that the intoxicated pigeon – which by the end of the trial everyone assumed had existed, except for the ex-police superintendent and consequently nine of his colleagues – could in fact have negotiated the descent down the chimney, nor that the chimney, at the bottom of which stood an electric fire, was negotiable even by a flea.

Billy advised it was strongly arguable that the learned assistant recorder had inferred that the burden of proof was on the defence, a most grievous misdirection. He further advised that a real pigeon, duly caged after consultation with the Royal Society for the Protection of Birds, should be taken to the Court of Appeal together with a can of Guinness.

'Why Guinness?' asked the instructing solicitor, as Steve when giving evidence had not specified his tipple or been cross-examined about it. Some specific beverage had to be selected, Billy replied; he himself preferred Guinness to other beers and felt that a pigeon would have a similar inclination, although he confessed he had no evidence on the point and had not consulted anyone versed in pigeon lore or lofts.

Opening the case before Lord Chief Justice Black, who said the case raised interesting points (he did not know how interesting they would become) Billy held up the caged pigeon, stating that here was the sole witness he intended to call. A frown could be observed on the learned Chief Justice's face.

'Give evidence? A pigeon? In what language?'

Everyone fell about. Lord Black was not noted for his humour but he was relaxing for a moment.

'Only metaphysically,' replied Billy.

Lord Black did not pick him up on this, being at heart a kind man.

'Jonathan will not go into the box.'

'Jonathan? Who is Jonathan?' asked Lord Black suspiciously. Jonathan was his own first name.

'Him, my Lord. Or her.' Billy held the bird even higher. 'As you mention it, which sex is it?' asked the judge, entering even further into the realm of merriment.

'Does it matter my Lord, except to another pigeon?'

Rolling in the aisles, even by those who knew the remark lacked originality. Billy then produced the can of Guinness from his trouser pocket.

The Lord Chief Justice looked at him in surprise. 'It is not usual, Mr Wickstead-Hacking, to take one's liquid luncheon refreshment in the courtroom during an appeal.'

'But this is exhibit two, my Lord. This lies at the root of the whole case. This – or one identical to it – is what made the pigeon perform such illogical manoeuvres on the night in question nearly two years ago.'

'Mr Wickstead-Hacking, this case is taking on an almost surreal atmosphere. Do let's get on.' Lord Black was becoming restive.

Billy took it that the judge wished him to give a demonstration. He opened the cage and tried to lift the pigeon out. The bird had other ideas, and one sight of the open door was enough to induce a break for freedom. It soared and settled in the cavernous roof of the majestic stone-pillared court of the Lord Chief Justice of England, part of the Victorian monstrosity in the Strand known as the Law Courts.

Lord Black was not amused. He thought Billy had done it deliberately. And his lack of amusement was increased when the pigeon – already partially inebriated by being force-fed Guinness during the pre-hearing conference between counsel, solicitor and their bemused lay client – decided to relieve itself while resting in the rafters. The resultant spat landed on the Lord Chief Justice's notebook, although he was too polite to take judicial notice of it, or even acknowledge its arrival. It was however borne in mind by him to question Billy's fitness for any kind of promotion in a note which was shortly transmitted to the office of Lord Chancellor Trotter's private secretary.

Such a missive from the Lord Chief Justice is normally fatal. Lord Black could make or unmake a barrister's career by a stroke of the pen. Billy did not know of this post-trial development, such matters being strictly confidential, but he had a shrewd suspicion of what might have happened. As he pressed on towards London at 55 m.p.h., the fastest the Volvo could manage, Billy reflected that if any such note had got into his file, Lord Trotter had been courageous enough to ignore it.

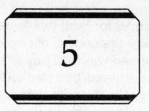

5

THE RIGHT Honourable Lord Trotter of St Pancras had never felt so isolated and depressed. The previous morning his wife, Lady Emeline Trotter, had had the whip hand and had held it over him for half-an-hour. She had not permitted him even to put on a dressing-gown. But she had let No-Knickers put her knickers on, together with the rest of her clothes, and slip downstairs to join Kingston in the office.

Meanwhile, Her Ladyship menaced her husband with the whip as he sat on his bed, stark bollock naked. She threatened to write a letter to *Horse and Field* magazine revealing all, unless he submitted to her demands. Trot was anxious to know what the demands were, and was initially relieved to discover that they had nothing to do with sex. Then he was plunged into deeper gloom when Lady Emeline revealed that she wanted money.

'What do women ever want?' said Trot bitterly.

Lady Emeline cracked the whip a few inches from his face, and he gave in. He knew she was serious about her threat concerning *Horse and Field*. She often wrote letters to its editor, usually in support of foxhunting, denouncing anyone who wanted to ban her cherished sport and calling for stiff jail sentences for hunt saboteurs.

The only other periodical of any kind that Lady Emeline ever read was the *Daily Telegraph*, and her husband was relieved that she had not proposed to write there. On the other hand, the readers of *Horse and Field*, although an esoteric group, were not sealed hermetically from the rest of the community. Any letter published in the magazine – and the editor would not dare risk a public horsewhipping by refusing – would soon reach the rest of the media.

So his lordship felt he had no alternative to signing over all his interest in the family home to her ladyship, together with £30,000 a year for her, for life. He did point out, as she stood over him, that the document to which he shiveringly put his signature was not a document of title, 'But you try saying that in a court of law,' said Lady Emeline menacingly. When she had what she wanted, she stumped out of the room, slamming the door behind her. Trot had never been gladder to see the back of her broad back and her even broader jodhpured behind.

Trot had had barely twenty-four hours to recover from this when he received the bollocking of his life from the Prime Minister about the latest antics of Nonie's incompetent husband. No wonder he was feeling low. He scanned the newspapers. The headlines told all. The affair at

Chandelle-Sweet's house was clearly an unmitigated disaster. He contemplated telling Nonie that from now on her duties would be exclusively secretarial, but where else could he safely achieve sexual satisfaction – of a sort – daily? He could sack Nonie and obtain a substitute, but there again there were problems. It was not thought appropriate for the Lord Chancellor himself to select his secretary – that was left to the number three in his Civil Service hierarchy, Annabelle Marrison-Smith, a Cambridge graduate with a first-class honours degree in psychology. She was generally thought to be a lesbian, as she had never married and always repelled sexual advances from the male staff as if she meant it, which she did. How could Lord Trotter tell Kingston to inform Marrison-Smith that she had to select a private secretary on the basis of big tits and readiness to engage in daily coitus with himself?

It would not look good in the careful minutes always kept on all official matters by senior civil servants. Besides, Marrison-Smith might refuse to co-operate or, worse, out of spite select as secretary another horse-faced lesbian like herself. Then, how could Trotter possibly sack Nonie unless he paid her an enormous sum to keep her mouth shut? A sum that he didn't have at the best of times, and certainly would not have now.

Trotter knew that his hour-glass was almost filled with sand, but he was determined not to surrender to that accursed man Slingsby. He felt like Hitler, launching the last-ditch Ardennes offensive in 1945 that nearly came off. But where

Hitler had failed, he, Trot, would succeed. Slingsby must not make that speech at Chesterfield. Trot would draft a final letter to the man and if that failed, any method of stopping him in his tracks, however desperate, would surely be justified.

A little later, the Lord Chancellor had second thoughts about Nonie. He sent for his private secretary and asked her what view she would take if she had to leave his service – if for example she were promoted to be private secretary to the Minister of Health? Nonie would have none of that. The Minister of Health was a woman and she much preferred to work for men, she told her employer, who already knew that perfectly well. Suppose then, he suggested, suppose that some event caused her to leave her present position through no fault of anyone's including her own. What sort of compensation would she look for?

'Fifty grand,' said Nonie smartly. Trot went a paler shade of pale. At that moment the telephone rang. It was Kingston calling to tell him that Eric Wickstead-Hacking had arrived. With relief, Trot postponed further financial discussions until he had seen his visitor.

Billy decided not to arrive at the House of Lords in his rusting Volvo estate-car. It was better to go there by taxi, as all taxis looked the same and did not reflect the worldly success, or otherwise, of their passengers. He might as well have saved the fare, however. The young lady with the Roedean vowels who appeared at the security desk to escort him to the Lord Chancellor's office welcomed him with frosty politeness. She had already assumed from a glance at his file that Eric Wickstead-Hacking was on the 'bollocking' list rather than the 'promotion' one.

This was confirmed by his appearance. He looked a bit like a genteel tramp after a wash-and-brush-up, she thought. She had to treat all visitors with impartial courtesy, but it was difficult sometimes. How could one talk to a low tramp in the same way one talked to a high Tory? (She was too young and naive to know that almost all tramps were Tories and more than a few Tories were tramps.)

Miss Roedean took Billy to the waiting-room and asked him to wait.

'I'm afraid there is only *The Times* for you to read,' she said, which grated with Billy. She was implying that he read lesser newspapers, which he did, but it was not for her to remind him. She added that it might be a little time before the Lord Chancellor could see Billy, as the Japanese ambassador was with him. Billy couldn't think what the two men could have in common, except they that they both wore funny clothes. After twenty minutes the Roedean lady returned and asked Billy to follow her.

And so he entered the Holy of Holies, the ancient panelled room, overlooking the even more ancient River Thames, in which so many destinies were decided. There decisions were made on judges to be appointed or promoted, honours to be conferred, famous people to be bollocked, the obscure to be made famous, and the pompous to be made even more so. What an important place indeed, what hallowed ground, how privileged Billy felt to be invited there by the Lord Chancellor himself, who sat at his desk in eighteenth-century dress – though to Billy's disappointment he was not wearing his long wig, which hung on a stand together with the grandest robe Billy had ever seen.

Trotter did not stand, nor did his private secretary Mrs Chandelle-Sweet who sat by him. Sir Anthony Kingston did stand and say 'Good morning', but he did not shake hands. By tradition barristers do not do this to each other. This is on the theory that hand-shaking was initiated to demonstrate that no weapon was concealed in the hand. Barristers-at-law being brothers in the law, and so above such treachery, do not need to demonstrate anything but mutual respect, which can be done without touching each other.

Lord Trotter forced a smile and indicated with a wave of the hand where Billy should sit – an unnecessary gesture, as the eighteenth century chair was placed in an obvious position in front of the Lord Chancellor's desk. Kingston put himself at his employer's right hand, an appropriate place, he felt. Mrs Chandelle-Sweet was on his left. Billy thought they looked like the three judges who sit in the Court of Appeal.

'Welcome, Wickstead-Hacking,' said the great man in the centre.

'Th-thank you Lord Chancellor,' stuttered Billy. 'I am glad to be here. It is a privilege, a rare privilege, which I do appreciate.'

Lord Trotter did not respond immediately, and Billy wondered if he had overdone it. But Trotter's momentary silence was due his inability to decide how to introduce his subject.

'This is a perilous mission that you are on, and, Wickstead-Hacking – or Billy, if I may – vital for the nation,' he began at last, in his most impressive manner.

Billy tried to hide his bewilderment. He must have missed something. Vital for the nation? It didn't make sense. Had he been mistaken for someone else? He'd heard that it did happen once, when a barrister was appointed to the High Court at the age of thirty-two, mistaken for his identically named father, when their two files were confused.

The father, aged fifty-four, had to remain at the Bar, even appearing before his son whom everyone, including the father, had agreed was in no way a chip off the old block, but rather a chip-on-the-shoulder young blockhead. But now people in the law pretended not to notice and even said, loudly enough for the Lord Chancellor and his permanent secretary to hear, what a brilliant young man the son was and what an inspired move to put him on the bench so early – the Treasury would get at least thirty-three years out of him instead of the usual fifteen or twenty. Barristers approaching the appointable age of forty-five to fifty said this especially loudly and often.

There was another pause. Then the Lord High

Chancellor started again. 'Look, Billy, no beating about the bush, eh? First let me say this. We are extremely grateful that you have taken the trouble to come all this way from that great Circuit of yours. I've always admired your lot down there.'

'Up' surely, thought Billy – north must be up.

'What great good people you've produced on the Northern Circuit. F. E. Smith, David Maxwell-Fife, Hartley Shawcross . . .'

'It's the North Midland Circuit, Lord Chancellor,' whispered Sir Anthony.

'I know that, Kingston. Of course I meant the North Midland. Slip of the tongue, that's all. Billy, you wouldn't be in practice when Shawcross dominated the good old North Midland?'

Kingston tried again. 'Northern, Lord Chancellor.'

'Yes,' Billy chipped in, 'but I am from the North Midland. Barfield chambers.'

Trot snorted. 'There you are, Kingston. Do get your facts right. We only have a limited time for this and we must press on.'

Kingston could not help himself: 'I'm afraid I must insist, Lord Chancellor. Shawcross was from the Northern, but Billy is from the North Midland.'

'I thought we had sorted that out already. Do stop being so tiresome, Kingston. You're just trying to confuse me.'

He hadn't come expecting to see the permanent secretary being bollocked by his boss, Billy thought to himself, but he couldn't help enjoying it.

'I'm sorry about that, Billy.' Trot was gracious in

victory. 'Now the reason I invited you here is this. You will appreciate that having been entrusted by Her Majesty with this high and responsible office, it is my duty to, er, keep tabs . . .'

Kingston interrupted. 'An eye, Lord Chancellor. Not tabs, but perhaps an eye can be kept.'

Trot stared at him icily. 'Are you sure you are feeling all right, Kingston?'

'Lord Chancellor, I was merely . . .'

'Pass him a glass of water, Mrs Chandelle-Sweet. Now, where was I?'

'High and responsible office.'

'Thank you, madam. Now Billy, the point is this. No beating about the whatsit, don't believe in that – straight to the point and no nonsense, every time, eh?'

'Yes indeed, Lord Chancellor,' said Billy dutifully, although he was still totally in the dark as to where all this was leading.

'It is my obligation to appoint, or rather advise Her Majesty about appointing, judges and so on.' At last the Lord Chancellor was saying something Billy could understand. 'And naturally, although I have to leave a good deal of the enquiries about candidates and so on to the Civil Service,' here he gave Kingston a withering glance, 'from time to time I conceive it to be my duty to see candidates myself, and this is one of those times. You follow?'

Billy was beginning to tremble with excitement, but he had to make sure. 'Lord Chancellor, I may have misunderstood, but when I last approached

Sir Anthony Kingston, I thought he said I hadn't a cat in hell's chance of becoming a judge.'

'Well, believe me, Billy, now you have.'

Billy still felt vaguely uneasy. There was an unreal atmosphere about all this. In fact he had to admit that the great man didn't seem entirely with it. He must have been overworking – all those files to read and judges to appoint or not, as the case may be. Poor fellows, the unlucky ones who were turned down – a fate worse than life. He congratulated himself on the phrase – he must try to use it in the interview, which at this pace looked like going on for days. Could he perhaps bring in 'Looking at life through a window of tears'? Why not? He'd have a go. What a coup, that, to boast about when he met his ageing pals at their weekly squash outing: games followed by pizzas in the local wine bar.

He decided to try and speed things up a bit. 'Lord Chancellor, you sent for me to tell me something. I assume it must be good news for me?'

'Well, Billy, one could say that, I suppose. We shall see.'

Now Billy was worried. If he was to be offered a judgeship, that was an odd way of referring to it.

'Let me put it another way, Billy. In this position that I have the honour to hold, one has to be very tactful and discreet. That's why we look to people like you.'

No one had ever said anything like this to him before, Billy reflected, but who was he to contradict the Lord Chancellor?

'I will be blunt, Billy. Several judges come from your great Circuit, the Northern.'

'North Midland,' Kingston interjected, quietly.

The Lord Chancellor ignored him. 'One of those judges from your Circuit is Mr Justice Slingsby.'

At last. A fact with which Billy could identify. 'He was in my chambers.'

'Precisely. We are getting to the heart and centre of this unfortunate matter.'

Unfortunate? That didn't sound good, thought Billy. Had Slingsby reported him again for some misdemeanour, as he had probably done after Judges' Night last year? On that occasion the visiting High Court judges and a selection of Circuit judges were being entertained at the Bar mess in Barfield. As usual, there was an all-in charge including drinks, and so naturally all the barristers competed to down as much as they could.

Alan Harrington-Smithurst QC, the small, thin, neurotic, bespectacled leader of the Circuit, was most anxious to join the bench and felt time was running out. He had spent ten days preparing his impromptu speech of welcome to the High Court judges, including a new judge, named Dyfed Lloyd Arswyl, who had joined them from the Wales and Chester Circuit.

Fortified with alcohol, the leader got up to make his speech. Unfortunately he had overdone the Dutch courage. 'We are extremely glad to welcome for the first time to our great Circuit the honourable Mr Justice Dyfed Lloyd Arsehole,' he blurted. This went down extremely well with everybody present except the judge in question. He could only manage a weak smile which definitely lacked sincerity.

Later, as the stretched Mercedes 300 containing Mr Justice Arswyl was about to leave the grounds of the Barfield Club, an unusual event occurred. The driver, Dicky Dickson, whose car this was – it was hired by the day as a sensible, though to some an irritating, economy – discovered that the air in all four tyres had been let out by some malicious person.

The judge was livid. His Celtic blood boiled loquaciously. 'Who the fucking hell can have done that?' he enquired, jumping out of the vehicle so quickly that he almost collided with dinner-jacketed Billy Wickstead-Hacking.

'Good evening, Judge, or is it good-night?' grinned Billy.

'What are you doing here?' queried Mr Justice Arswyl, crossly.

'Taking the air, judge. Yours has been taken already, I see.' Billy gestured to the deflated tyres.

'Did *you* do it?'

Billy laughed. 'Where's the evidence, your Lordship?'

'Answer the question.'

'I prefer to take the Fifth Amendment, your Lordship.' Billy, who had nothing to do with the prank, thought the whole thing was a huge joke.

Mr Justice Arswyl did not. 'Don't be an idiot, man. At least do something to help.'

'What do you expect me to do?' slurred Billy. 'Blow into your tyres?'

Exasperated, the judge jumped back into the Merc. and angrily demanded that Dicky get rid of this drunken oaf who was standing outside the car. Next day he reported Billy to Mr Justice Slingsby, who told Billy to watch it and be more circumspect in future. But, Billy now wondered, had Slingsby also sent a note about the affair to the Lord Chancellor for his file? Billy's thoughts jerked back to the present. 'What was your Lordship saying about Raymond Slingsby?'

'He has ability of course, but he can be very difficult in some ways.'

Billy was only too happy to agree. 'We found that in chambers. He insisted on ridiculous things, like giving every member of chambers a vote on who we should take in as new people. Is that the sort of thing you mean, Lord Chancellor?'

Trot was grave. 'Much worse than that, I'm afraid. You've seen this dreadful fuss about Judge Chandelle-Sweet?'

'We all have.'

'And your attitude?'

'I agree with you, Lord Chancellor.' Billy wasn't clear what he was agreeing with but the sensible thing seemed to be to go along with the man who had all the power.

'May I take you into my confidence, Billy?' Trot leaned forward.

'Oh, every time, absolutely,' said Billy eagerly.

'Raymond Slingsby is proving to be a very real embarrassment to the whole judicial system. In fact embarrassment isn't a strong enough word.'

'Dangerous?' offered Billy.

The Lord Chancellor smiled. 'Nail on the head, Billy. Splendid. The man has to be stopped before he destroys the whole system. Revolution, fighting in the streets.'

Billy looked worried. 'Where is that going on, Lord Chancellor?'

'No, no, Billy. I'm looking ahead. Thinking what could happen if something isn't done about Raymond Slingsby. That speech he proposes to make next week at Chesterfield. He must be stopped from making it.'

'But aren't you the man to do that, sir?

'Not as easy as that, I'm afraid. There's an Act of Parliament. High Court judges can only be removed by both Houses of Parliament.'

Billy was puzzled. 'But how can I help you?'

At these words, Trot pounced. 'That's exactly what I wanted to hear. How you do it, Billy, is your affair.'

'Do what, Lord Chancellor?'

'Help us.'

Billy felt he was adrift again. Why did the Lord Chancellor talk in riddles? Was it a trap? 'If you could specify, sir – what you want me to do.' He tried to look intelligent as he said this, but found it hard.

'Silenced. The man has to be silenced,' said Trot firmly.

'I see, Lord Chancellor. But how – how is he to be silenced?'

'Entirely a matter for you, Billy. It's for you to find a way to shut Slingsby up. In the interests of the nation.'

Billy felt proud in a vague way, but why couldn't the Lord Chancellor be more specific? 'I see,' he said slowly, playing for time, 'but if you could just give me a few more details . . .'

Trot waved his hand in a dismissive way. 'The details are for you to decide, Billy. We don't want to know. But your country will, of course, reward you should you succeed.' He stood up. 'Remember, Billy, you must close the mouth of another, while also keeping your own tightly closed.'

'I see,' said Billy again, but he didn't, not clearly. The interview was over, obviously, and though he longed to say those two words, 'Circuit Judgeship?' he couldn't force them out. Moments later he was on the pavement outside the Palace of Westminster, wondering what the hell to do next.

A certain promise was there, he was sure of that, and it was worth having a go to assist 'them' to the best of his ability. As he drove north on the M1, jerkily, since the faithful old Volvo was losing faith in itself at last, an idea was already germinating. He did not now feel as confident that a gleaming new Volvo 850GLT would soon be his, but if his mission – Operation Slingsby – did succeed, it would surely stand outside his house before long. He would get his judgeship – at least that's how he read the enigmatic signs coming from Lord Trotter, now that he had time to think them over.

The only problem was that Raymond Slingsby was his friend, or had been until he rose to the High Court, and that troubled Billy a bit. But duty must come before friendship; nobody could deny that. It is better to betray one's friend than one's country – where had he read that? Ray Slingsby only had himself to blame – he had rocked the boat and alarmed the captain and crew. He should have known that it can't be done and got away with.

So there was a lot to do and it had to be done quickly. Billy was still in the 'up' phase of his cycle. He was feeling great, functioning well and in his present mood he could tackle anything, but the downward turn could come in the next week or so. He must see Janet Yorke again, as soon as he got back to Barfield. Janet could be the vital link in the chain between himself and a new Volvo, via the come-uppance of Mr Justice Raymond Slingsby, a socialist and a High Court judge – an impossible combination, as those on the North Midland Circuit had said ever since Slingsby's surprising elevation to the bench.

Janet welcomed Billy with arms that were open and legs that were soon to be opened. He was hungry for more than food, and so was she. Before eating the meal she had prepared, they sated their sexual appetites like wild beasts at breakfast. They tore off each other's clothes – easier for him, as she was not wearing much more than a pungent passion-arousing perfume which soon performed its intended task.

Billy had wide experience of wild ecstatic flings, and Janet's age was in his experience the best in a woman. Virginal inhibitions had gone and he had no need, with a woman of her maturity, to overcome maidenly hesitation. The way was soon open, the keeper of the way signalling entry with open lips and bra-less boobs that invited kissing and caressing. A woman who was around thirty knew what to do without being instructed or cajoled. She knew her body and how it responded, and she could without embarrassment wordlessly but clearly indicate the path to passion and pleasure.

Ideally both should arrive at their common goal together. Billy was good at that, and women, including Janet, appreciated it. She had even wondered if, in spite of his faults, Billy might be the man she had searched for and never found in any of the TV producers or other men who had come and gone and mostly come too soon and not gone soon enough. One day he would arrive, gently leading and caring, but not Billy, no – once the afterglow of passion died away, Janet was realistic enough to know that except in bed he was a dead loss.

The trouble was that Janet was still a romantic, despite everything, all the hopeful false beginnings and bitter endings. She felt that she had, in both senses of the word, been had by so many, but she still believed that one day she would close the book and sign the register for the final time. Even though the gales of time had already flicked over many leaves of her life's calendar, and she sometimes wondered how many more were left to be turned.

As a television presenter, Janet gave herself nightly to a million men. They wrote and phoned

North Midlands TV and sent gifts and letters that expressed deep devotion and the wish to do things that did not attract her. At least not with men she did not know or want to know, though their wanting to know her fed and flattered her ego.

Unclothed and sated, she and Billy sat up in bed, thankfully an ample double one. Billy poured from the bottle of Bulgarian Gewurztraminer that Asda were offering cheap. He always bought wine when on a sexual forage, as he was also, as even he could not help realising, a bit too fond of a drink. Though he must watch it from now on – it would be ironic to have a new Volvo 850GLT and be banned from driving it.

Billy felt good, really good. Even at fifty-nine he was getting better at sex and Janet had enjoyed it, genuinely, he was sure, more than any woman he had had for a long time. And that made it much better. He wondered if she was falling for him. It would be very flattering, although he had no wish or intent to reciprocate – he must concentrate on Operation Slingsby.

'Darling.' It slipped naturally from his tongue when talking to any woman he had bedded. 'I think we can go places together.'

'I hope so Billy. I do like you. I really do.'

For a TV presenter she wasn't all that good with words, Billy thought, but which woman can have everything?

'Come to Ireland with me next weekend,' he said out loud, in his most caressing tone. 'It's your weekend off, isn't it?'

Janet, who had just taken a gulp of Gewurz-traminer, almost choked on it in surprise. Up till now the most Billy had offered her had been the cut-price special in the local Pizza Hut. 'Ireland? Why Ireland, Billy?'

Billy snuggled closer. 'It's so romantic. A friend of mine's offered me his cottage in West Cork. You'd love it there – the Gulf Stream, palm trees, wild fuschia hedges. Time doesn't matter, but people do. It's a great place, Janet.'

Intrigued and attracted, but still hardly able to believe that he meant it, Janet demanded more details. Billy explained that they would fly from North Midlands to Cork and pick up a car there. He said the idea was to make up a foursome with another couple he knew. It would be a terrific party, he promised her.

This was where Janet began to have reservations. She thought she knew what Billy's idea of a foursome would be and she didn't like it. She'd tried it once, but while changing partners and watching the other couple had the attraction of novelty, the thrill of discovery, a good one-to-one situation was warmest and best. You knew where you were with one. With two couples it was just a bit kinky and it grated against the Nonconformist strain that she must have inherited from her northern forebears – all Methodists and stone-masons.

Billy could see that Janet was not going to play along with him without good reason. There was no alternative to telling her his plan then and there, though he had hoped to delay it until they were on the plane. He explained that he had been entrusted with a patriotic mission to save the judiciary and that this had possible rewards for them both. Mr Justice Slingsby was proving to be a disaster, a danger to everybody connected with the law, and the Establishment had to get rid of him. Billy's bright idea was to get him to Ireland with a bimbo and to take compromising photographs of them there. When the photographs were published, Slingsby would be disgraced and would have to resign. The simplicity and brilliance of this plan had startled even Billy himself. As far as he could see, provided he could persuade Slingsby to come to Ireland with him, it was foolproof.

Janet's role would be to take the photographs. She could well get a lucrative story out of it, perhaps even a book, and she had always wanted that. Billy did not tell her about his hoped-for judgeship: unadorned patriotism sounded better than naked ambition. But Janet knew Billy well enough to assume there must be more in it for him than he was revealing. You didn't work in TV for as long as she had done without gaining a certain insight into the way people's minds work.

Janet was perfectly aware that what Billy was suggesting was a low trick, but when she thought about her huge overdraft and her ever-increasing mortgage arrears she had to admit that she was tempted. She was also professionally intrigued by the idea of getting a story on Mr Justice Slingsby – he was newsworthy, a powerful personality, someone quite out of the common run. Trapping a High

Court judge could not be considered honourable, but it was the kind of thing that went on these days. Though she felt an undertow of guilt, why should she not take advantage of Billy's offer?

She asked who the fourth person was, the bait for the trap. At this point Billy had to confess that he hadn't found her yet, and that he hoped Janet would be able to assist. There wasn't much time, as his intention was to take the six-fifteen flight to Cork on Friday evening. They would return on Sunday evening and everything would be on him, he said grandly – fares, booze, meals, the lot. Janet would have nothing to do but enjoy herself and take a few photographs.

In for a penny, in for a pound, thought Janet, running through in her mind the attractive single girls of her acquaintance. Suddenly she had the ideal person – Sarah Garrowby. Until recently, Sarah had been a Page Three girl. Now she was twenty-four – old for that job – and she was trying to get into acting, pantomime, anything that would extend her career. She wasn't a tart. Most Page Three girls weren't, whatever men assumed when they met them at parties, all dressed up – or dressed down. Men thought they'd be on to a good thing with Page Three girls, but willingness to sell their image to a million men did not mean the girls would sell or give the real thing to more than one select man at a time.

Sarah had a fellow she lived with, but she had told Janet she was feeling restless and a bit fed up with him. She was ready for a change there as well as a career move. Billy agreed that she sounded ideal, if Janet was willing to try her.

Should she tell Sarah what the trip was all about and her role in it? asked Janet. No, Billy decided without thinking, not at that stage, or Sarah might be put off. It would be better to tell her when they had left England and there was no turning back. He would decide when and how to explain everything, if indeed it proved to be necessary at all.

They would have to play it by ear – Billy's favourite method. That way you did not have to apply much grey matter in advance. It was best to tell Sarah it was a fun thing, a weekend of drink and relaxation with Janet, a High Court judge and a barrister. While anything could happen, she was not committed in any way. It was a sort of blind date, with trimmings.

Janet agreed that was the best approach, and she was right, as a phone-call to Sarah soon confirmed. Sarah sounded excited by the idea. She had heard of Mr Justice Slingsby and thought he seemed a good sort, a bloke she would like to meet. Billy was already congratulating himself on the success of his scheme when he realised they had yet to rope in the key person – Ray Slingsby himself. If he wouldn't play, the trip was off. Perhaps Billy had done things the wrong way round. He did tend to do that, rushing off at a tangent impulsively, building castles that turned out to be sand-castles, soon washed over by the seas of chance. But he would press on and see how things went. He picked up the phone and rang the Judges' Lodgings. Operation Slingsby was under way.

6

H̲ELEN SLINGSBY was puzzled, as she told her husband when he returned from court still dressed in scarlet-and-ermine, in the Merc, escorted by a police car and two motorcyclists with blue lights flashing. Why should Billy Wickstead-Hacking want to come and see Ray, saying it was urgent? She had never liked that man and he had a terrible reputation with his drinking and womanising. Then there was the pigeon thing and the chambers dinner – one never knew what he would do next.

Ray found Helen's attitude irritating. He had had a tiresome day in court and in spite of all his brave words, the Trotter business was beginning to get to him. His speech to the Chesterfield magistrates was looming ever closer and he was committed to going through with it, but even he could not avoid a slight tremor of anticipation at the thought of the inevitable catastrophic row that would follow.

Helen was so po-faced sometimes. Billy was harmless enough really; a bit mad but he couldn't help it and when sober he could be excellent company. They hadn't always agreed when they were in chambers together and Ray was head of chambers, but Billy had been a bit of light relief. The poor chap didn't seem to get a lot of work these days – in fact Ray felt quite sorry for him, though he had to admit that even now Billy did seem to get some fun out of life. And he couldn't help secretly envying him his success with women.

Billy parked the Volvo in a street near the Lodgings. The faithful old car wouldn't have looked impressive if it had presented itself to the policeman at the gate and parked by the Mercedes or some other posh car. There were social distinctions between cars as between people. Besides, the ageing Swede could have refused to start and having to ask the police for a push-start would not be dignified.

Helen tried to be polite to Billy and almost succeeded, though there was an underlying coolness in her manner. Billy knew she didn't care for him, but that was common with gentrified county ladies. They were not his sort, and he was not theirs. After two whiskies for each man, a small dry sherry for her and some light Circuit gossip, Helen left Ray and Billy alone in the plush drawing-room. What a grand life the judges had, thought Billy, admiring his surroundings.

The thought spurred him on to broach the subject of his visit. He began by telling Ray that he had been hoping for some time to see more of him. They had hardly met since Ray left chambers for the bench. It had also occurred to him, whilst seeing Ray in court this session, that he was looking a bit strained and peaky. He wondered if he might benefit from a weekend away playing golf, because it so happened that he, Billy, was just about to go on such a weekend with two friends. There should have been fourth member of the party, but he had dropped out at the last minute. So there would be room for Ray to join them if he cared – in fact he would be doing Billy a favour. He'd have a good time, Billy could guarantee that.

'I know what your idea of a good time is, Billy,' said Ray. He was undeniably attracted by the idea of a quiet golfing weekend, but he couldn't help wondering if that was all he would be letting himself in for.

'You mean booze?' Billy asked.

'And floozies.' Ray though of Helen's comments earlier.

'All right then, I enjoy myself,' said Billy defensively. 'I like having a good time. What's wrong with that? What's life for? Nose to the grindstone till you get your nose in the grave?'

Ray smiled in appreciation of a phrase that for Billy was outstandingly good. He'd probably polished it for some jury, and stored it for re-use thereafter.

'Is that what this weekend is all about, Billy? Drink and women?'

Billy was glad to note that Ray wasn't condemning the notion out of hand, but inquiring almost as if it intrigued him.

He grinned. 'I must admit that the two other

members of the party are lady friends of mine. Terribly nice girls – I know they'll be thrilled to meet you. One of them's a secretary and the other does some clothes modelling.' He had decided in advance that he would not reveal Janet and Sarah's real jobs at this stage. A Page Three girl and a TV journalist sounded a bit much to swallow, even for a man as sex-starved as he suspected Ray Slingsby to be. Slingsby would probably find out what the girls did sooner or later, but Billy hoped and trusted that it would not be until they were safely in Ireland, by which time he would be committed to the trip.

'And where are you going, Billy? Scotland, I presume.'

He must be interested, thought Billy. He took a deep breath because he knew the next bit could be tricky to get over. 'No,' he said, 'Ireland, actually. A friend of mine's offered me his cottage in West Cork. There's some great golf there and we could even do a bit of fishing.'

Ray looked disappointed. 'But you know judges aren't supposed to go to Ireland without getting the Lord Chancellor's permission, especially if they've done IRA cases, as I have. Trotter would say no, bound to.'

Billy summoned all his persuasive powers. 'We don't tell him. There are no passports required for Ireland, and if anybody wants to know, you are John Smith or Snooks or anything you like. Wear dark glasses if you're afraid of being recognised. Besides,' he knew this would be a telling point, 'you're not going to tell me you care about anything old Trot has to say to you.'

This was true enough, but Ray was still dubious. 'It's all a bit cloak and dagger, Billy. And anyway, let's face it, no I can't, I really can't. I'm a High Court judge, and I'm married. It's asking for trouble. It's madness.'

'Ray, you've been on the Bench for – how long?'

'Three-and-a-half years.'

'Another fourteen and you can retire. But you'll probably go on till you're seventy-two and by then you'll be clapped out and good for nothing that's enjoyable. Life is for living, Ray, and you never really have lived, have you? Admit it.'

'Well, I don't know.' Ray Slingsby pondered, more tempted than he cared to admit.

'You may never get another chance, Ray. The offer's open – now it's up to you. I'll expect to hear from you by tomorrow lunchtime.'

Pre-dinner drinks at the Lodgings began at 7.15 as always and dinner was timed for 8 p.m. as always. Life at the Lodgings had a routine that in its essentials never changed, whichever judges were there. The senior judge made all the main decisions, seniority being the guiding principle of the schools they had attended, the Bar at which they had formerly practised and the judiciary that they graced in appearance and sometimes disgraced in fact, though few barristers dared to say that openly.

Careers would be dented, appointment to the bench denied and promotion blocked, by a casual word spoken in the small whispering gallery that was the Bar and bench of England and Wales. The domestic decisions for the senior judge – then Mr Justice Paul Tinkering, a bachelor – included who should be invited for dinner and whether to invite the Bar and their wives to a cocktail party – not too often as it was expensive and there were limits set by the Treasury, as well as by reluctant judicial unbending in the supposed interest of good relations. No one really wanted good relations with some of those deadbeats, but when a party for the Bar was held they all had to be invited plus their 'ladies', which in practice included live-in lovers (how the Bar of England and Wales had fallen from its once proud place at the head of social and professional life, thought Mr Justice Tinkering). It also included 'friends', thought by the counsel concerned to be better so described than mistresses. No-one could prove anything, not beyond reasonable doubt. There was also the odd sister, usually very odd.

It had been suggested that Henry Halsing-Forde, the only member of the Circuit to have openly come out as gay – he was wealthy and neither had nor needed much work from solicitors – might be permitted to bring his lorry-driver friend. But Mr Justice Tinkering drew the line at that. That was how ancient Rome had fallen, wasn't it? – circuses and sodomy – though as a mathematician by training he was vague about the details.

Another decision for the senior judge was whether to 'dress' for dinner. Tinkering was in favour of 'black-tie' every evening, but after a long involved dispute with Ray Slingsby – who was very persuasive on the point – he compromised, saying he wished to be reasonable, though Ray thought that if he was being so it was an entirely new but welcome departure. It was agreed that dinner jackets should be worn on Monday and Thursday evenings and whenever an official guest, as opposed to a personal friend, dined. Official guests included the High Sheriff, Lord Lieutenant or Deputy Lord Lieutenant and the Mayor. In each case they brought their wives and none had ever asked to bring as consort anyone not so described. They would cross that rickety bridge if and when they had the misfortune to arrive there.

That evening the High Sheriff, Sir Arbuthnot Darling, and Lady Darling were official guests for dinner. The office of Sheriff was ancient; he represented the Queen in the County and as the High Court judges were Her Majesty's judges he acted as their host in theory. He sat on the bench in court on the first day of the judicial sittings, when the quaint Norman French commission was read, while all stood, having been bidden, by the clerk to the judge trying crime, to be silent on pain of imprisonment. Then 'Know ye by these presents ... a Commission of Oyer and Terminer and general gaol delivery ... saving unto us the amerciments from thence to us accruing ...' Ancient dogma that meant nothing by then except that the British – the English especially – were wedded to the past as firmly as the Pope was wedded to the Church, and to tradition that some said gave life to our land and others said would yet bring death to it.

That is what Ray Slingsby was pondering as Sir Arbuthnot and his lady, both beautifully clean and gleaming, came in. The scene had not altered since Victorian times, except that then the men would have had beards or at least moustaches and sideburns. Norman, the little butler, and Mary, the big waitress, glided around with sherry on silver trays. Mr Justice Tinkering was observed to have a large gin and tonic with ice – he refused to drink sherry saying 'It rots the gut'. But though he mentioned this to the guests he never offered them a choice. The Empire itself was built on this unconscious disregard for the interests of others.

Slingsby scorned all this protocol nonsense, but went along with it as part of the job. He was too polite to hurt the feelings even of those who daily trod on the feelings of others. He observed with interest the mannered, affected small talk between supposedly important people such as senior judges, Sheriffs and Mayors. He regarded them, most of them, as toffee-nosed twits; he did not reveal in their presence that he thought that, but did wickedly accurate impressions of them in their absence, though only to a favoured few.

Sir Arbuthnot had been flattered to be selected by the Queen when the office of High Sheriff for North Midlands was being 'pricked' for, but he was not certain what that process involved. HM was said to have three names put before her, picking the winner by pricking his name in some way, on the parchment on which the names were written. Whether she did it with a pin or a needle, no-one knew. Did she do it blindfold or with her eyes open? If blindfold, who guided her pen and wasn't he in effect selecting the appointee, using HM as a mere instrument? If HM kept her eyes open, on what basis did she choose between three mere names, or were potted biographies attached to them?

In any event no-one would ever find out except HM and her top civil servants, none of whom was likely to talk to the *Sun* or the *Courier* or even *The Times* about it. Sir Arbuthnot thought it must be a bit of a farce because he had been told months previously that he was a cert for the job, though he mustn't breathe a word to anybody except his wife, his secretary and his cat (he added the last bit when telling the story after his election).

Sir Arbuthnot's father, Sir Ernest Darling, Bart, made a fortune by building up the Darling-Dearest shipping line. His own name was Darling, but he had induced his co-shareholder Tom Else – a practical man who had earned his position because he knew how to make ships whereas Darling only knew, or thought he knew, how to make money – to change his name to Dearest, for publicity purposes. They could then proclaim that the company was run by two men who not only put their real hearts and souls into the business but their real names too. This went down well with journalists short of copy, and financial journalists short of ideas, and the company never looked back until Sir Arbuthnot succeeded his father.

Arbuthnot knew nothing about ships or making them, but did know about money and losing it, particularly at roulette. He had gone to Stowe school and afterwards to Egbert Hall, a small Oxford college. The college was reluctant to take him until his father donated £250,000 to endow a chair on merchant navy law confined to graduates of Eggy Hall. It then decided to look again at Arbuthnot's A levels – an E in Art and a U in Woodwork. The college fellows in solemn conclave decided it would be wrong to be influenced by father's generous gift, which, however, they had no intention of returning. Nevertheless they resolved that academic ability was not the only consideration in a prospective undergraduate; character came into it too.

True, Arbuthnot's Oxford entrance examination papers showed a certain deficiency in spelling, but such lamentable shortcomings were general in these unregenerate days. In the history paper Arbuthnot had answered only one question, writing thirteen lines in the course of which he confused Henry VIII and Edward VIII, stating that the former was wrong to divorce Mrs Simpson for being an American and chiding Edward VIII for chopping off Anne Boleyn's head in order to 'detract' public attention away from Adolf Hitler. The examiners passed this off as signs of a rare sense of humour, and the college, indeed the country, badly needed that increasingly rare commodity, so they accepted young Arbuthnot and the Professor of Merchant Navy Law was duly appointed.

At the age of thirty-two, Arbuthnot succeeded his father as second baronet and chairman of

Darling–Dearest. At thirty-three he was promoted to president of the company on his written undertaking to take no further part whatever in any of the company's activities except the annual dinner and dance for senior management, when he could announce the dances.

Arbuthnot had been an ideal choice for High Sheriff. He had a title and a famous name, knew all the social notabilities and liked dressing-up in knee-breeches, buckled shoes and ruffle. He also had just about enough money left after touring the casinos of Europe with a foolproof system that only proved what a fool he was.

Lady Darling, from the upper-crust Spenimore-Cressington brewing family, was that rare being in the English aristocracy, a woman with common sense. She had managed to persuade Arbuthnot to put his remaining money in trust, with himself as beneficiary and a solicitor and retired accountant as trustees. The solicitor was a man small in stature and mind but large in reputation. He had the manner of a knowledgeable person and was known to be a sensitive man, because whenever he was discussing anything difficult with his clients he burst into tears. This distracted those in conference with him, and the point at issue would be passed over in favour of concern for his health. The accountant was eighty-four and ga-ga, but between them the trustees were more reliable than the beneficiary, so the trust was a move in the right direction and the loss of capital was stemmed.

Conversation at the Lodgings that evening was made easy for Arbuthnot, for he had earlier in the day been sitting on the bench in Ray Slingsby's court.

'I say, that fellow in the shirt was a bit of a whatnot, eh, Slingsby?' he began in a hearty tone.

It always annoyed Ray that this nitwit should address him by his surname, but he let it pass, as he had done on several previous meetings. He thought the reference to the man in the shirt on the vague side, but let that pass too. Drinks time was not a time for talking seriously, but for drinking seriously.

'How are the ships then?' Ray ignored Arbuthnot's inept conversational opening and tried one of his own.

'Ships?' Arbuthnot looked blank.

'Your shipping line. Darling Deer Park or whatever it's called.'

'Dearest,' said Arbuthnot firmly. He was at least sure of the name of his company.

'I beg your pardon, I'm a little deaf.' Ray was in a mischievous mood.

'DEAREST!' shouted Arbuthnot at the top of his voice.

The whole room heard it, and Helen Slingsby was most concerned. What on earth had been going on between her husband and this dreadful Sheriff man? Surely this couldn't be the reason why Ray had not touched her sexually for four-and-a-half years except to peck her cheek or pat her hand, if those gestures could be called sexual?

She did not regret the end to all the distasteful touching and groping, when Ray had wanted to do things that she found alien and alienating. Mouths were intended for eating and talking, for social and not for sexual interplay, but even Ray, nice considerate Ray, had been influenced by all this modern talk about sex and how enjoyable it was and how everyone had to get as much of it as they could.

Helen was convinced, and had been from the time her boarding-school spinster teachers told her carefully and austerely about what happened between men and women, that sex was for procreation not recreation. She and Ray had produced a nice child in Anne, and they had intended to provide a brother or sister for her, but somehow the sexual urge between them had withered and died too early.

Now it was Mr Justice Tinkering's turn to converse with the High Sheriff. The judge had very little small talk and preferred to block all balls solidly, letting them bounce back with their own unspent momentum. He rarely initiated conversational ploys.

'Fascinating job, yours, Tinkering, eh? By jove, yes, fascinating, eh?' said Arbuthnot, doing his best.

'Can be, I suppose.'

'Do you like putting on the black cap?' asked the High Sheriff brightly.

'Never done it.' Mr Justice Tinkering looked rather wistful.

'You don't believe in hanging, eh? It's a jolly good thing, that's my view. Keeps down the riff-raff, eh?'

'Indeed,' said the judge, declining to elaborate on his views.

'I bet it makes the beggars sweat, eh, dangling on the end of a rope.'

'I would imagine so.'

'Just the thing to wake them up, that's what I say.'

Mr Justice Tinkering was mildly surprised that the High Sheriff seemed to assume we still had the death penalty, but it was against his principles to argue with a guest. He made a heroic effort. 'Like *your* job do you, High Sheriff?'

Arbuthnot looked bewildered. 'Which one?'

'How many jobs have you got?'

The High Sheriff thought for a moment. 'Only this one, now,' he said gloomily.

Tinkering had had enough. Using the accepted ploy for killing a conversation on such occasions, he said his glass was empty and edged away, ignoring Sir Arbuthnot's remark – a sensible one, for once – 'But I say, drinks'll be coming round again in a minute, won't they?'

Mr Justice Tinkering knew there was no bar at which to replenish his glass with tonic water, which was always his choice as a refill, but he was a tactful man, having been trained as a Chancery lawyer in Lincoln's Inn, where all humanity was firmly forbidden to enter. Chancery lawyers were black-suited men and the occasional black-dressed woman. Most of them went into court only rarely, preferring to pore over conveyances, trust deeds, wills and ancient Trustee Acts. They devoured steadily and with intellectual satisfaction what normal individuals found not only boring but indigestible.

When appointed to the High Court, Paul Tinkering QC had not been assigned to the Chancery Division, where there was no vacancy, but to the Queen's Bench where they dealt with big-time crime, civil actions arising out of accidents at work or on the roads, and contract cases. He knew nothing about such work except what he dimly remembered from distant student days. But that was no hindrance in the eyes of the Lord Chancellor's office, where they were concerned with filling judicial vacancies rather than with finding suitable candidates. Tinkering was an ace mathematician, and the theory was that such men could master any subject by applying brain-power to it during a weekend. Those who appeared before him were not all convinced of the soundness of such theory. He did not seem to understand machines in factories, preferring to concentrate on the refinements of the Factories Act and the concatenation – his word – of regulations made thereunder, contrasting one with another and finding distinctions that were intellectually stimulating though unrelated to the facts of the case he was purporting to try.

In crime, which he had been taught to treat with disdain – it was too sordid and too simple for minds like his – he was even more at sea. Once, when hearing a case of bestiality, he asked the young prosecuting barrister whether penetration was alleged to have been *per anum* or *per vaginam*. Tommy Smithson was too young ever to have studied a word of Latin, so he was not only unappreciative of Mr Tinkering's deftness with Latin case endings, but had no inkling at all of what the question was driving at. In his confusion and not wishing to expose the ignorance of which he was conscious, he answered 'Yes'.

'Surely it must be one or the other, Mr Smithson?'

'Or both,' commented Tommy, desperately.

'Both *per vaginam* and *per anum*? Are you sure? The prosecution statements, which I have perused most carefully, do not appear to confirm that. Is there evidence I have not had placed before me?'

Tommy was in a thickening fog, and a real dilemma. If he said there was further evidence, the judge would require to see it. If he said there was no further evidence he would contradict himself. He took the only way out and said he wasn't feeling very well, which was true, and would his Lordship please grant him a short adjournment. It was nearly twelve-thirty, so the judge, who was feeling hungry, was pleased to adjourn till two o'clock. Tommy rang his clerk and told him to send someone else to take over the brief, preferably someone who had studied Latin. He himself intended going abroad for a short holiday – hopefully to Italy where bits of useful Latin might still be lying around for all he knew – to consider whether he was fitted for the law. He was never seen again.

Mr Justice Tinkering was saved from hovering foolishly while looking for a bar that didn't exist, when his Worship the Mayor of Barfield,

Councillor Derek McMahon, arrived. He introduced a completely different element to the company. The Mayor was one of 'them'; not one of the educated rulers but a member of the uneducated class, who had to be tolerated because without them who would drive buses and empty dustbins? Derek had himself emptied dustbins and still did when not released for mayoral duty, which the privatised concern who employed him were pleased to do. As they depended for their existence on a contract with the local authority, they felt it could do no harm to be on good terms with its titular head, who presumably had some pull by virtue of his position.

Now forty-nine, Derek McMahon had joined the Transport and General Workers' Union at twenty-three and given them service that could be called consistent rather than useful. He always attended meetings and followed the official line, as he understood it. When the Union was very left-wing so was he, visiting Moscow several times on official union delegations and making speeches that even those of his Moscow comrades who spoke perfect English had difficulty in understanding, though they politely clapped every incoherent sentence, to show international solidarity.

So often did Derek visit the USSR, where the hospitality for foreign Communists was outstanding – caviare for the General Workers' Union – that he had been suspected of being a crypto-Communist. That was without foundation. Derek could not distinguish Karl Marx from

Harpo, but the suspicion was increased when he came across an old Left Book Club volume in a second-hand bookshop. Thinking its contents were still official Labour Party policy, he learnt them almost by heart, parroting phrases at Union and Party meetings and impressing the sleepier delegates with what they thought were his original thoughts eloquently expressed.

At the age of twenty-six Derek was elected to Barfield council. It was noted by the discerning, who did not tell him, that his popular vote was most popular in areas where he had not canvassed and exposed his full personality on the doorsteps. He was much better on paper than in the flesh. At all subsequent elections, when he was elected each time with dwindling majorities, the party bosses convinced him that canvassing was for the others and that it was more important for him to be in the committee-rooms where the election was being organised. So he visited them assiduously, loquaciously urging them on with excerpts from the Left Book Club volume, now held together with Sellotape.

On the council, Derek's main aim – undeclared to his closest colleagues, though they could guess – was to be Mayor and chief citizen. It was a great honour to be selected. There was the gold chain with all those names on it, and so heavy that it required the services of a mace-bearer to carry it when not placed with dignity on his undignified shoulders. Then there was the Mayor's official car, a Jaguar, although once Derek became Mayor himself he pressed the council to invest in a Rolls-

Royce. It would increase the prestige of the city, he said – not that he personally cared what sort of a car he rode around in.

'Then get him a mini,' the leader of the minority Tory group impishly interjected at a council meeting. Derek loftily ignored this, largely because he couldn't think of a reply. Barfield should have a Roller, so that he could arrive at other towns in style and put them in their place. Unfortunately he had not succeeded in convincing the council that this main plank in his policy was justified, and they still had the decrepit Jaguar.

In spite of this disappointment, Derek enjoyed being Mayor. He especially liked meeting other civic heads. They formed a select mutual admiration society, inviting each other to their Mayor's Days and Mayor's Balls. Only cities could join, of course. You could not mix with mere boroughs and certainly not with parish councils, perish the thought. When a reporter asked how he squared this disdain with socialist egalitarianism he asked what that was. He then did some research in the Left Book Club book and concluded that the best line was as follows. He believed in a classless society, but we had classes that could not be abolished immediately. They would be eventually, but in the meantime the class struggle had to be intensified – discreetly – people would not vote for you if you told the truth. The intensified class struggle would then in the long run – the very long run, hoped Derek – overthrow 'the system'. He did not know what that last bit meant but it sounded good.

His Worship the Mayor was delighted that his title put him on first-name terms with people he would never otherwise have met and who would certainly never have let him call them by their first names, if he had remained a mere public-health attendant. This was what bin-emptiers were now called. He *was* somebody, and so was his wife Freda, a machinist in a factory where they made underwear.

When he found himself talking to the Mayor of Barfield, Mr Justice Slingsby's mind was on other things. This offer of mad Billy Wickstead-Hacking's – it attracted him, in spite of the fact that he knew he would be crazy to accept it. He glanced across and saw Helen chatting pleasantly to Paul Tinkering; she was doing most of the talking. She could talk to anybody whoever they were, from the Prime Minister at the top to this new Mayor of Barfield, who by some standards was as far down the social scale as anybody could be.

Helen had so many fine qualities. She had been a good mother – kind, loving, giving, wise. Firm when necessary but always understanding. That was why everyone liked her and why he did himself. He had pursued her and married her for her goodness. She had not a wicked, nor even a selfish thought in her, and yet here he was, seriously contemplating spending a weekend with another woman.

She would never understand it, thought Ray, but if she did find out she would probably forgive him. Although he knew that she would never encourage him to look for gratification elsewhere, he could not help wondering if she would altogether mind as long as he did not desert her, always came back, healthy and whole, and did not disgrace her – no appearances in the *Sun*, the *Courier* or the other terrible tabloids.

Security and stability – that's what she wanted. Did all women feel the same, Ray asked himself. Was it inevitable that they should lose interest in sex – at least with their husbands – once they had had their children? The trouble was that he had only his experiences with Helen to go on, and her interest had never been more than tepid even in the early days of their marriage.

Whereas he had always been interested in sex – what man wasn't? What healthy man never thought about sex, never wanted it, never dreamed, day-dreamed, built up pictures of an ideal warm no-holds-barred relationship with a willing, thrilling breasty young woman? An all-systems-go, functioning at all levels relationship, an all-consuming, exploring and searching and finding and renewing relationship. But would it ever happen?

This wild scheme of Billy's – the more he thought about it, the more tempted he was. But what if he did go, and was found out? How could an innocent interpretation be put on his presence? Even if the whole weekend did turn out to be entirely innocent, which was always possible, though knowing Billy's reputation he somehow doubted it.

Then what about the women themselves? What

were they expecting? What were they like, come to that? Perhaps 'his' girl wouldn't care for him. Perhaps he might not even find her attractive.

What was the morality of it? What duty did a husband owe to his wife not to stray, once sex between them had ceased? Should he deny his nature, causing frustration, even anger and resentment towards his wife? Ray had been brought up a Methodist, though he had long ago ceased to have any real belief in religion. But he had absorbed the ministers' teachings during his childhood, and he knew that they still had an effect on him to this day. Wasn't it centuries of the Christian church, with its fear of women and sex, that had caused all the hang-ups? For centuries they taught that there should be no sex between a man and a woman except when they were married to each other.

Ray was brought up to believe it and he still had the feeling that one man, one woman for life was right. But was it? Could it be that simple? If you were not religious, what did it rest on? If there were children, it was easy. Parents had an obligation to stay together for their children's sake – he had seen what happened when that did not happen, in custody cases when pathetic kids, asked which parent they wanted to live with, said 'both', bringing tears to his eyes.

On the other hand, if there were no children or they had reached puberty or beyond, was there the same obligation to stay with one's spouse? It could only be based on a moral contract. A woman like Helen had done her part in looking after the house and bringing up the children, and the husband was therefore morally bound not to ill-treat her by abandoning her without reasonable grounds. But could abandonment be said to include temporary playing away, especially if she didn't know about it? Everybody else seemed to be up to it these days, and an awful lot of men, and women too, got away with it.

The Mayor was saying something and Ray tried to concentrate on his words in spite of the battle raging within himself. Big Mary came round with the sherry tray and hovered hugely before the Mayor.

'Oh, it's my turn, is it? Took your time getting here, didn't you?' Derek examined the contents of the tray with a discontented expression. 'That all you got? What about a beer?'

The man's ungracious manner grated on Ray, but he was a guest, after all. 'Whatever you like, Mr Mayor.' He nodded to Mary and she departed for the cellar. Ray could tell that it would not be the first mayoral beer that day.

Derek looked round the room. 'Nice place you've got 'ere. I've been 'ere before, you know.'

This was clearly a significant remark, and Ray took his cue. 'Have you, Mr Mayor?'

'Aye, I have, and you'll never guess why – I've emptied your dustbins.'

'No, really?' Ray feigned astonishment that he did not feel, as he knew perfectly well that the Mayor had been a dustman.

'Aye, somebody's got to do it.' Derek sighed deeply. 'It's a capitalist world, sithee.'

'Who does it in a socialist world?' asked Ray, really curious to know.

Derek laughed. 'Not me, judge, I'll tell you that. Nobody's going to exploit me, not any more. Not on your life. Them days has gone.'

'You don't look exploited, Mr Mayor. You look quite prosperous. And I was reading in the *Clarion* about you wanting a Rolls-Royce.'

'That's not for me, oh no. That's for the workers.'

'Will they ride in it?'

'Them that'll be Mayor will.'

'All pigs are equal but some pigs are more equal than others,' Ray could not resist quoting. It seemed especially apposite in view of the Mayor's decidedly porcine appearance.

'Eh? What?'

'It's something George Orwell wrote.'

'Does he live round 'ere?' asked the Mayor suspiciously.

'He doesn't live anywhere. He's dead.'

'Bet he was exploited, I shouldn't wonder.'

'Orwell was an Etonian.'

'You all are, aren't you, you posh barristers and judges?'

'I went to Barfield Grammar School, Mr Mayor,' Ray was delighted to be able to inform him.

'Snobby lot, them. I went to Battinson Secondary Modern.'

Fortunately the beer arrived in time to save Ray who, for once, was at a loss for words. The Mayor took a long draught.

'That's better. That's what I call a drink. None of

your fancy sherries for me, I'm a man of the people.'

'The people must be very grateful.' Before he had finished the sentence Ray knew he shouldn't have said it. He was becoming like the rest of the judiciary, from whom he had tried to distance himself. The Mayor wasn't such a bad fellow, just a bit of a chump like most politicians. Ray shouldn't talk down to the man – not all that long ago they had both been in the Labour Party. Ray was still left-wing, at least that was how he thought of himself, but was he being sucked into something else, imperceptibly? His attitude to the Mayor made him wonder.

The butler came in, went to Mr Justice Tinkering and spoke a few quiet words.

'Aah. Dinner is served,' the senior Judge announced.

'Just a minute,' the Mayor called out, holding up his hand. Everyone stopped chatting and looked at him. What on earth was the man going to say now?

'Just a minute, before we go into wherever we are going, I'd just like to say a few words, as the senior citizen of this great city of ours, Barfield. It's a real honour to be amongst you lot, it really is. And you're very welcome in our city, you judges and people. Thank you very much.'

'Thank *you*, Mr Mayor,' Ray murmured insincerely.

Mr Justice Tinkering said nothing, his thoughts being unrepeatable.

* * *

The following morning, Lord Trotter's last-ditch letter to Ray was delivered to Barfield Judges' Lodgings. The black crest on the back of the envelope and 'Judiciary in Confidence' on the front told Mr Justice Raymond Slingsby it was from the Lord Chancellor. Opening it with a feeling, soon confirmed, that the sender might be resorting to extreme measures, Slingsby read:

My dear Ray,

You and I have not known each other well, though our paths have crossed from time to time in this great profession in which we all naturally retain feelings of fraternity all our lives.

I write to you now so that, if it is at all possible, a situation which cannot be in the interests of either of us, can be avoided, and we can both pursue our separate careers with future possibilities of progress retained, or enhanced, in each case.

It would be pointless of me to rehearse all that has happened in our respective and mutual spheres during the past year or so. Suffice it to say, I regret such animosity as may have entered our dealings, as I feel sure you do.

*I make no accusations, for that would serve no purpose except to intensify any bad feelings that may have arisen between us. I make no promises and expect none from yourself. **But I do feel and I am confident that such is reciprocated by you, that present animosities must now be ended permanently.***

Between grown men in a great profession, this is surely not impossible. But this I emphasise with all

*my heart: unless we are both prepared to withdraw
accusations, one against the other, of impropriety of
any kind, disaster looms.*

*You may not have intended it – indeed I accept
that you did not – but in some of your recent public
statements there has been a certain tendency, which
anyone however humble can surely detect, to
indicate that I have acted with less than due
objectivity and honesty in my dealings with others.
There has even been detectable by some, hints that
my private secretary and I may have been less than
professional in our relationship. Believe me, any such
hints or references may be genuine in intention but
are wholly unfounded in fact.*

*In clarifying matters generally, I am prepared to
do anything practicable. I will make any statement,
give any promise and further any endeavour. But
please understand that if all else fails, then I may feel
it incumbent upon me to bring the unhappy
situation to an end in the only way open to me in the
case of a High Court Judge – pursuant to the
Supreme Court Act 1981.*

Believe me, my dear colleague, to be
Yours ever
Oswald Trotter

The bullshitter, Ray said to himself. If he meant
'Shut up or I'll have you sacked,' why not simply
say so? He would not be threatened like this, he
thought – it was the final straw. His quick temper
getting the better of him, he grabbed a pen and
rapidly scrawled a reply on Judges' Lodgings
headed notepaper:

Dear Lord Trotter,
I received your letter.
And I think you'd better
Quit
You shit
Yours never
Raymond Slingsby.

That would shake him, he thought savagely. He knew that with this letter he was almost certainly about to wreck his career, but at that moment he couldn't care less. He addressed the envelope, sealed it up and threw it on the post table. Then he picked up the telephone and dialled Billy Wickstead-Hacking's number.

7

THE GROUP of four sat at a table in the departure lounge of North Midlands airport, ready for the flight to Cork. The Honourable Mr Justice Raymond Slingsby – as he had no wish to be known at that time – sat next to Page Three girl Sarah Garrowby. Barrister Eric Wickstead-Hacking was on the opposite side of the table with TV presenter Janet Yorke.

Before leaving for the airport Billy had telephoned Sir Anthony Kingston, told him of the plan and arranged to send a message as soon as Operation Slingsby had been carried out successfully. Billy and Janet had decided not to reveal the secrets of the operation to Sarah: she might cry off and then all would be lost.

Ray felt uneasy. The wave of anger and defiance that had led him to take up Billy's invitation was ebbing away and he was beginning to wonder what he was doing. He had naturally scorned Billy's idea of disguising himself with wig and dark glasses, but he was wearing a black felt hat with a wide brim which covered his balding head, and his new Burberry raincoat had a large collar which, when turned up, partially covered his face.

From under the brim of his hat, he studied his female companions. They were both very attractive, and the moment Billy introduced them he had felt a pang of guilt on Helen's behalf. She had been so nice when he had told her about Billy's invitation. A quiet golfing trip was just what Ray needed, she said, and it was very thoughtful of Billy Wickstead-Hacking to invite him. Perhaps there was some good in the man after all. She had been a little concerned when Ray had revealed they were going to Ireland, but he had assured her that it would be fine and because she trusted him, she believed him.

That feeling of guilt intensified when he looked at Sarah Garrowby. She was a very pretty girl with long fair hair curling loosely on her shoulders and big, innocent grey eyes. She wore a short skirt which showed her long, shapely legs and a close-fitting blouse emphasised her firm, ample breasts.

Would he have the chance to examine those breasts more closely? thought Ray. The idea gave him a deliciously guilty feeling. He knew it was forbidden territory but he would like to trespass on it. He must go easy however, no rushing, nothing clumsy or intimidating. There must be no repetition of the disaster with the German girl.

Ray wondered why Sarah was there. How had Billy got hold of her and what did she see in this weekend jaunt? She seemed quite intelligent – no empty-headed bimbo – which surprised him, because he had always suspected that models were a bit stupid. He wondered if she enjoyed her job, and he looked forward to finding out more about it.

He thought Janet seemed a bright girl too. He was taking less interest in her because she was obviously Billy's partner, but it had struck him when they were introduced that there was something familiar about her. Not so much her face as her voice – he was sure he had heard it before somewhere recently. It was partly the familiar Barfield accent, of course, but there was something more to it than that.

He dismissed the thought. It wasn't important, and anyway, he was far more interested in enjoying Sarah's sweet smile, her moist and generous lips, the quiet laughter in her eyes. He only hoped he wouldn't screw things up with this warm eager-looking young woman, towards whom he already felt predatory yet protective.

At twenty-four, Sarah felt she was at a crossroads. Ever since she was in her early teens, friends had said that with her face and figure she should become a model, and at sixteen she left school with five GCSEs and took a modelling course. During it, she was talent-spotted by an agent who saw her potential as a Page Three girl. Sarah worked hard and things came good for her. During her best period she earned up to £500 a day – not bad for a girl still in her teens. But now she was older, things were tailing off. The *Sun* no longer took her, the *Courier* not very often. She still modelled clothes and there should be work in that for a few more years, but she had never hit the bigtime. She often asked herself what it took to do that – but she only knew that she didn't seem to have it. Ordinary models like her were two a penny – well, she was a little bit more than ordinary, but not all that much. It was time to move on, but to what?

Sarah's live-in boyfriend of six months, Simon, was a photographer. Simon wasn't a bad chap, though a selfish lover. There were rows, and she certainly didn't think he was Mr Right, but he was good-looking, strong, he laughed a lot, and everybody had to have somebody.

Sarah first met Janet when she was inter-viewed by her after a fashion show. She was wearing a new see-through dress which showed her nipples and caused a sensation, as the designer had intended. The two girls hit it off immediately and after the show went out for a drink together. They found they had several things in common, especially men problems. Men were always the main problem: they were selfish and inconsiderate, most of them, and could not be trusted.

Sarah had not mapped out her future very clearly, but she thought she would like to get into acting. You needed more than a good face and figure, though, and so far she had turned down any propositions from theatrical agents as likely to lead to the casting-couch rather than the stage. Her own agent said there could be a small part in pantomime next Christmas, but there was nothing definite in it yet. If she did get a toe on the stage, she might meet the right man – not sleazy-fingered agents and photographers, but a real gentleman with money and a position who would love her and protect her.

She thought this judge seemed interesting, even though he must be about the same age as the father who had left home when she was twelve. He also seemed shy. According to Janet he was married but separated and on the point of divorce – she wouldn't have come otherwise. Janet said it would be a fun weekend with no strings and Sarah was happy to go along on that basis. But why the hurry, the short notice? It didn't seem to make sense, and she couldn't help wondering if there was something more to it than had been revealed.

She didn't entirely like the look of Billy, or trust him, though Janet said he was all right and she should know. Anyway, Sarah reassured herself, this judge wouldn't be going if there was anything shady about the trip, would he?

Billy was feeling very pleased with himself. The plan was going better than he could have hoped. Ray had taken the bait after initial hesitation, and within hours the trap could be sprung. In a way he was sorry he had to do this to someone he had known quite well for many years; not a close friend but a friend all the same. They had had some good times in chambers and there had been a real sense of fellowship – helping each other with their cases, especially in the early days, discussing points of law and amounts of damages, except of course when they were on opposite sides in a case.

That was the strange thing about life at the Bar. You were both allies and opponents, living with colleagues who shared the same set of rooms and the same all-powerful clerk, who handled dealings with the solicitors who sent them work, or didn't. Billy had never had as much work as Ray, and he had to admit that this had caused a measure of resentment, which made his present task a little easier.

There had been memorable celebratory dinners when a member of chambers became a QC or a judge. The dinner for Ray was a great occasion and Billy made the key speech, which went down like a dream, or so it seemed as he was making it. He was not so sure when he woke up with a devastating headache next day and recalled the disapproving looks of the ladies present – three members of chambers and a dozen wives, girlfriends or whatever. He should not have let his trousers fall down. It made a point, but not – so far as he recalled – the one he intended, though he could not remember what that was.

Helen Slingsby had raised her eyes to the ceiling in silence, but some of the other women had been more vocal and several had used words such as 'disgusting' and 'disgraceful'. They were too narrow-minded. It was only a bit of fun, and on the whole the evening had been a success, a worthy tribute to a worthy colleague, despite his nonsensical socialist notions.

It was a pity their friendship had come to this, thought Billy, but Ray should have had more sense. He had himself to blame and no-one else.

He had tried to challenge and beat the system, and it could not be done. It should not even be attempted because the Lord Chancellor – whatever one thought of the man himself – had a position that should be respected. To set out to topple the person who headed the whole legal system was not only arrogant but verged on treason, and if Billy ever had to justify what he was now embarked on he would not shrink from that word.

Ray had had his warnings, his chances to halt, and by pressing on in his forceful heedless manner – so typical of socialists – he had been walking into a minefield, knowingly. Whose fault was it if he got blown up? It was sad, of course, because no-one could call Ray Slingsby corrupt, he was just wrong-headed. He meant well, in a way, but to accuse the Lord Chancellor of corruption ... Anyway, there it was. They were on their way now and events must take their course.

Janet Yorke, sitting beside Billy, wondered why you always waited longer on the ground for a plane than you spent in the air. As they waited, Billy went off to buy another round of drinks. Booze, she thought, looked as if it would play a large part in this venture. Each of them already had a plastic bag bulging with bottles. Billy had told them what to buy, and it seemed to her to be enough for a dozen weekends.

She hoped they wouldn't all die of alcohol poisoning – that would be a wonderful story for TV, though she had no wish to provide it for someone else, and especially not for Zoë, the new young blonde that 'Currant Affairs' had just taken on. Zoë seemed eager to take over Janet's job, but it would be over her live body. She hoped the drink was not more than the Irish allowed, but according to Billy they allowed almost anything and were the nicest, most charming people he had ever met anywhere – though not perhaps the most efficient.

This was a peculiar enterprise in which she and Billy were engaged, Janet said to herself. She still wanted to get to the top in her chosen field, but trapping an honourable and nice man – as Judge Slingsby seemed to be – was not the worthiest of missions. But, she rationalised as she had done so often before, a journalist had to get the story, by any means available, because the public had a right to know, and that had to come first. People often resented the way she told their stories, she knew, but that was just too bad. However decent they seemed, the truth was more important than their feelings. Besides, she needed money – badly – and though this job might not be nice it would be lucrative.

Janet felt a strong desire to check the small Olympus Superzoom fully automatic camera that she had carefully packed in her case a few hours earlier. She must ration her drinks from now on. She knew she was too fond of alcohol, which she often resorted to as a cushion against life's disappointments, especially those in the shape of men. The moment her camera had caught Judge Slingsby and Sarah in a compromising position, she was to drive to Cork airport in the hire-car,

166

leaving the other three isolated in the cottage, with Billy playing the innocent. Meanwhile, she and the film would fly to England on the first available plane. The *Sun*, the *Courier*, or the *News of the World* would pay telephone numbers for those photographs, she thought. She had promised to leave Billy out of the scenario and she would do her best, but it might prove impossible. At the end of the day, the story was paramount.

Finally, the flight to Cork was called. As they walked across the North Midlands tarmac carrying their clinking plastic bags, Mr Justice Raymond Slingsby felt reasonably confident that so far he had not been recognised by any passengers, airline staff or stray media persons. Two pretty, smiling young Aer Lingus stewardesses welcomed them aboard the small Saab SS 340 prop-jet plane. It could take thirty-nine passengers, but on this flight half the seats were empty.

Ray sat down beside Sarah and fastened his seat-belt. He couldn't help wondering how such a toy-like aircraft could lift itself into the air at all, but when the pilot put the two turbo-props into frantic thrust the tiny eager plane belted across the runway and – just in time, it seemed – left the earth for the air.

Sarah, who hated flying and avoided it when she could, looked at Ray and smiled in a relieved way. Ray, who often flew and thought no more of it than catching a bus, smiled back at her in reassurance and fleetingly touched her warm hand with his. She did not flinch or frown, and Ray's heart leapt with excitement.

In London late that same Friday afternoon, Lord Chancellor Trotter was in his flat. He was tidying things up for the weekend with Mrs Chandelle-Sweet, starting with his trousers.

Trot was feeling more buoyant than for some time. Billy had rung from the airport to say that everything was on course, and that Slingsby seemed to have swallowed the bait. By now they should be well on their way to Ireland. Wickstead-Hacking's scheme was most ingenious, he thought. Others must have underestimated the man, and he could prove to be an inspired choice for the Circuit bench when a vacancy arose on the North Midland, as could happen soon.

On Mr Justice Slingsby's expected resignation the Lord Chancellor had in mind promoting to the High Court a Circuit judge, Alex Battinson, who had worked hard at the Bar and on the bench, valiantly overcoming the twin handicaps of state education and a foreman plumber as his father. He deserved recognition, and Billy Wickstead-Hacking could take his place. Eyebrows might be raised; there could be comments in the press, but let them publish and be damned. No-one had to approve his choice and no-one could question it effectively, even in Parliament.

Trot's euphoria improved his performance in bed no end. He made it to the winning-post for the first time in weeks, with No-Knickers cheering him on.

'You're feeling more cheerful, Trot,' said Nonie, as he rolled off her with a smile on his face.

'It's looking good, Nonie. Billy rang earlier, while you were out of the office. This weekend should see it all wrapped up.'

Nonie frowned slightly. 'The PM gave you till Monday evening, didn't he? Billy had better work fast, otherwise you'll be for the chop.'

'It isn't going to come to that,' said Trot confidently.

'How are you going to use the photos, if you get them?'

'*When* I get them. As soon as Slingsby knows they're in our hands, he's bound to resign.'

'If he refuses?' Nonie was not completely convinced. She thought Mr Justice Slingsby might be made of sterner stuff.

'Then the tabloids'll lap them up.'

'You're going to gloat when he resigns, aren't you?'

'I shall feel quiet satisfaction.'

There was a pause. Then, 'I can't help feeling sorry for that man,' said Nonie.

Trot was aghast. 'Nonie! Why?'

'He's right about my husband being useless. And about us. I've only met Ray Slingsby once,' she went on in a voice that held a hint of wistfulness, 'but I bet he's good in bed.'

Trot laughed. 'I hope he is, and I hope he gets stuck in good and proper over there.' He did not register that Nonie was reflecting unfavourably on his own performance, which might have satisfied him, but certainly hadn't satisfied her.

'Then step forward his Honour Judge Wickstead-Hacking, I suppose,' said Nonie, without enthusiasm.

'Could be.' Trot smiled. He had to be patient for just a few hours longer, but he had every confidence that Billy would pull it off.

The Opel Kadett was waiting outside friendly little Cork airport, and Billy took the road through Kinsale – not the shortest route but scenically the best. They passed the marina full of big yachts from England and France, halyards clanking against aluminium masts. They drove through the narrow streets with their quaintly painted shops and cosy restaurants, then on via Bandon and Clonakilty, which in the seventeenth century boasted they had no Roman Catholics within their walls, and now held very few who professed any other faith.

There was little traffic on the road. Ireland was as underpopulated now as it had been since the 1840s famine. The only hold-up came when they passed a church where a funeral was in progress. In Ireland everyone has to go to a funeral – it is social death not to attend – and the road outside the church was jammed with cars, tractors and donkey-carts.

They drove down to Rosscarberry and crossed the causeway that divides the town square from the unspoilt sweep of sand and sea that is the locals' beach. In the square, they stopped outside the Shamrock Hotel.

'How about a drink?' Billy asked his passengers.

Now he was here, he wanted to take things slowly, as the Irish did. There was no need to rush; the calmer and more casual everything was, the better. Ray Slingsby seemed to be enjoying himself, he thought. He looked far more relaxed, now he was away from England and possible prying eyes. Billy was also glad to see that Ray was getting on well with Sarah. They were talking about her job now – she had told him that she was a model who wanted to become an actress, and Ray seemed genuinely interested. Billy couldn't help being pleased that Sarah hadn't said anything about being a Page Three girl. He had asked Janet to indicate to her, in the nicest possible way, that a judge mightn't totally approve of this aspect of her career and that it would oil the social wheels if she played it down. Even at this late stage, there was still an outside chance that Slingsby could be frightened off if they didn't tread carefully.

Roy Kelly, the Shamrock Hotel's genial landlord, chatted to the group as they downed their half-pints of frothy Guinness – with some difficulty in the case of the two women, who soon graduated to gin-and-tonics. When Roy asked where they had come from, Billy said 'England.'

This did not surprise Roy. 'Which part of England?' he asked.

'The north,' said Billy vaguely. He didn't want to be too specific, but his evasiveness only roused Roy Kelly's curiosity. The landlord was genuinely puzzled by this group – they seemed such an ill-assorted bunch. The man in the spectacles could be from the City, but the little fat man looked like a bookie's runner, though he had a posh voice. The elder of the two women might perhaps have a job in finance – she looked a competent sort – but the young blonde was a mystery. She seemed to be with the tall, bespectacled man but she had no wedding-ring, so she clearly wasn't his wife. Perhaps she was his bit on the side – he didn't look that type, but you could never tell these days.

It crossed Roy's mind that they might be underwriters, insurance men or estate agents – the sort of shady 'money' people who got their finances mixed up with those of their clients and went in for yachts, fast cars and fast women. He decided he would like to know more about them. It made life a bit more interesting on a Friday evening in sleepy Rosscarberry.

'Been to Ireland before, have you?'

'No,' said Billy. There was an awkward pause. 'But it's nice,' he added. He felt this was very feeble, but it would have to do.

Roy probed further. He had the quiet persistence that makes licensees in any country the repositories of both valuable intelligence and useless information.

'Come to fish, maybe, have you? A lot of you people come here for the fishing.'

'Not fishing, exactly,' Billy said, and laughed. Roy Kelly glanced at Ray Slingsby and smiled, and Ray tried to smile without looking embarrassed. Roy gave a slight wink, and an invisible thread of sympathy was spun between the two men.

172

He thinks I'm a man of the world, thought Ray. If only he knew.

'So it's not fishing that you've come for exactly,' Roy persisted.

'Golf, actually.'

Roy thought it odd. The fat one had said it wasn't fishing as if he had almost, but not quite, hit the nail on the head, but what did fishing and golfing have in common? Fishing was done by solitary men – you didn't see many fisherwomen – and golfing by gregarious gadabouts of both sexes. Anyway, they weren't dressed like golfers, and he doubted if the blonde had ever held a club in her life.

'Must be a problem, bringing four sets of clubs in a small car like that one out there, and you with the luggage to put in it, and all.'

'We're going to hire them.' Janet felt that she couldn't stay silent any longer.

'And at which club are you planning to play these games of golf, then?'

Billy detected a tinge of mockery in Roy's voice – not malicious but distinct. He jumped to his fat feet and said he was sorry to break off the interesting conversation, but they were a bit pushed for time and had some arrangements to make. As the four left, Roy glanced out of the window and made a mental note of the car number, which he then wrote down on the back of an envelope.

Sarah was worried. 'Do you think he rumbled us, Ray?' she asked as they drove away.

'What is there to rumble?'

'You're an English judge. You're not supposed to be here. He could be a member of the IRA.'

'No, Sarah – he's not the type at all,' said Ray. He was trying to reassure both himself and the others, but when it came down to it he hadn't a clue how you recognised an IRA man except that they were usually young – as Roy was not – and dark-haired.

'We've done nothing wrong,' Janet said, trying to make light of things.

'Not yet,' said Billy, and laughed loudly.

Ray glanced sideways at his companion. He felt excited but also a bit guilty and more than a bit apprehensive. Would he botch the whole thing, as he had done in Germany? Would he misread Sarah's signals and jump the gun? Would he find the gun wouldn't fire at all, if the opportunity arose? He was sliding into a world he wasn't equipped for. There were risks, imponderables, dreadful possibilities as well as potential delights.

He could put an end to it now, tell Billy to stop the car and let him get out. It would be easy enough to ring for a taxi in Rosscarberry and return to the airport or stay the night in a Cork hotel. But the moment passed and he said and did nothing, and soon the car was out on a deserted country road again – they were very near to the cottage now, said Billy.

All four of them liked the look of the old cottage that had once been a small farmer's house. It was reached by an unmade lane and you could not see the building from the road; it was hidden by high

174

hedges of wild fuchsia. Ray thought the location ideal. Even if the media had been on their trail – and he told himself yet again that he had no reason to suppose they were – they would not find the house easily, unless the O'Donovans at the adjoining farm and small shop told them.

Matronly Annie O'Donovan and her sixteen-year-old twins Flo and Teresa tended the shop from 9 a.m. to 9 p.m., seven days a week. As most locals called in for groceries and petrol or diesel – there was one pump for each in front of the shop – Annie was the intelligence centre and knew everybody and what they were up to. She held the keys to the cottage and looked after it for the owner, who had told Billy to make sure he had Annie on his side, and all would be well.

Soon they were sitting outside the cottage in the evening sun, sampling the 'duty-free' goods they had brought. There was blossom on the half-dozen fruit trees in the cottage's front garden, and about a quarter of a mile away was a lake, visible from where they were sitting. Ray said he'd like to go and look at it tomorrow, and Billy said it would be a pleasant walk, but secretly he thought there might not be a tomorrow if all went well within the next few hours.

After sitting and chatting for half an hour, while the gin and whisky levels lowered, the delicate question of who was to sleep where was organised by Billy as tactfully as he knew how. There were three bedrooms upstairs. They were separated only by wooden partitions, so that sounds carried. He allotted the bedroom at the far end of the corridor to himself and Janet. It had two single beds which could easily be pushed together. Nothing had been explained to Ray about Billy's relationship with Janet, but the familiar way in which they talked and acted required no explanation.

Billy gave the middle room to Ray; it had a single bed. Sarah's was to be the room at the other end of the corridor. It had a double bed, and Billy felt confident that Ray would soon be sharing it. Everything he had so far observed between Ray and Sarah happily pointed in that direction.

The bathroom was downstairs, apparently carved out of the kitchen during some improvements in the past, but the loo was at the far end of the corridor by Billy's and Janet's room. This produced a noise embarrassment, but who cared? They weren't there to practise niceties of etiquette, Billy told himself, but to have a good time, and more.

It was getting late now and everyone was hungry, so they set off in the Opel for Castletownsend, about six miles away, where young, genial and bearded Stephen O'Driscoll and his nice wife Sile owned and ran the Castle Bar. This ancient hostelry was on the street that ran down to the harbour, past two trees in the centre of the road bounded by a circular wall. There had been trees in this inconvenient spot for hundreds of years, and the locals had decided not to disturb them. When the original trees had to be removed because of age and disease, two more were planted in their place, and traffic still had to circumvent them, though Guinness had caused more than one motorist to come into conflict with the protective wall. Billy managed to avoid the wall on their way down, but Ray wondered if he would be able to do so by the time they went home.

They sat in the old bar with its low wooden beams and pictures and photographs on the walls, drank more whisky and gin and ordered dinner. This was taken upstairs in a small room with a view of the yachts tethered in the bay and the rocky headland beyond. Ray thought that this was the sort of place he would like to live after he retired at sixty-five, and he said as much to Billy. If only he knew, he was likely to quit the bench much sooner than that, thought Billy to himself.

Before they went up for dinner, Stephen O'Driscoll asked if they had come far. From the English Midlands, said Billy. And was it fishing they were after, Stephen wanted to know. No, golf, Billy told him, deciding to stick to the tale he had told Roy Kelly in Rosscarberry. Stephen said he had thought Billy looked more like a fisherman and Billy couldn't resist saying that he was not a fisher of fish but could be called a fisher of men.

'Ah, a priest, perhaps,' said Stephen with a smile. They all laughed heartily at the absurdity of the thought, but when Stephen thought about recent news reports of bishops and priests and their extra-cathedral activities, he wondered if it was really so unlikely. At any rate he, like Roy Kelly before him, sensed that there was something odd about this English party.

Where did they propose to play golf, he asked. Glandore, Billy told him. He felt it was better to name a course rather than say they had no idea, and he thought that there was a golf course at this attractive little harbour not far away. But though he did not say so, Stephen O'Driscoll knew there was no course at or near Glandore. Billy had mentioned to him that they had called in at the Shamrock Hotel earlier that evening, and while the four dined he made a quiet phone-call to Roy Kelly, with whom he played golf every Wednesday afternoon.

Dinner was delicious. There was fresh seafood to eat and three bottles of Nierstein Bereich to drink – chosen by Billy who claimed (falsely) to be a connoisseur of wine – followed by Irish coffee and brandy. Ray knew they were drinking too much but said nothing. All four were talking away like old friends. Ray kept his companions entertained with true anecdotes, while Billy amused them with untrue ones. The women laughed at them all impartially.

Ray knew it was mischievous, but he could not help mentioning Billy's famous 'Case of the Inebriated Pigeon', which had given his colleagues in Barfield so much enjoyment. Billy laughed ruefully and said that it was a bit hard that one of his most famous cases was the one that had probably put paid to his chances of promotion forever. He could afford to laugh, he thought to himself, because it almost certainly wasn't true any more.

Janet, whose normal sharp acumen had

deserted her after their evening's drinking, couldn't help chipping in, 'But at least some good came out of it, Billy. Don't you remember, we met when I interviewed you for Channel 6 about it?'

The moment she had spoken, she could have bitten her tongue out. The expression on Ray's face told her that her cover as a secretary was blown good and proper now.

Of course, thought Ray, how stupid could he have been? On television – that was where he had seen, or rather heard her before. And she had actually interviewed him – she had been the presenter in the London studio for the debate with Trotter and Chandelle-Sweet. No wonder he had thought he had heard her voice before. And if that bloody monitor had been placed where he could see it, he would have recognised her long before.

'Billy,' he said accusingly, 'what the hell are you playing at? You told me she was a secretary, not a TV presenter. I'd never have come if I'd thought you were bringing a journalist along.'

Billy thought fast. Never had he needed to sound more plausible. He grinned and tried to look unconcerned. 'I'm sorry Ray. I admit, I misled you. But then you've said yourself you wouldn't have come if you'd known about Janet's job – and aren't you glad you did come?' he added, glancing meaningfully at Sarah. 'Besides, Janet's not a reporter, she's a presenter – there is a difference, you know. And she's here because she's my girlfriend, not for any other reason. Isn't that so, darling?'

'Of course.' Janet smiled at Ray in what she

hoped was a reassuring manner. 'I really am off duty this weekend, I promise. I just want to enjoy myself and relax – and I'm sure you do too.'

Ray allowed himself to be convinced. After all, he was here now, and there was nothing he could do about it. And Billy was right, he was enjoying himself – more than he had done for as long as he could remember, if he was honest. The truth of it was, he didn't want to leave the party, even if he could find a way to do it. And he certainly didn't want to leave Sarah.

The talk flowed on. Only at one other stage did it take a more serious turn, when Billy began to denounce the IRA and blame them for the trouble in Northern Ireland. Ray said it wasn't as simple as that – he could understand the attitude of nationalists who resented what they saw as British occupation of part of Ireland. Billy became heated, taunting Ray for soft socialism amounting to treachery. Loudly but illogically he went on to assert that the Birmingham Six and Guildford Four had been guilty, and they should have been blown up by their own bombs. Embarrassed, Ray tried tactfully to steer the conversation into calmer channels. Billy's remarks could be dangerous if overheard. Some people might draw the wrong conclusions.

Billy finally calmed down, and Ray was distracted from his concerns by the realisation that Sarah's leg was accidentally – or was it? – resting against his. Had she realised it was there, he wondered. He smiled at her and she smiled back warmly.

He was a smashing bloke, Sarah thought, regarding him through a haze of drink. She wouldn't mind going to bed with him even though it was normally against her rules on a first meeting. Her usual tactic was to play it cool and hard to get, but maybe she could make an exception in an exceptional situation. She only had two nights available, after all, and then perhaps she'd never see him again. That altered the rules of the game.

In her mind she felt Ray's sensitive hands on her boobs and his lips tenderly, patiently on hers, showing real respect, real affection, not grabbing or forcing – she hated men who did that. And then, and then . . . Sarah was moist already, and all at once she could hardly wait to get back to the cottage for the serious business to start.

Could Ray help her to get on the stage? He had influence, he was bound to have, and he said he liked the theatre, talking about it as intensely yet knowingly as he talked about everything. It was hard to accept that he was fifty-one. But what did age matter, if two people really liked each other?

Ray had not banished all feelings of guilt entirely, but he was trying hard. This was his opportunity, he told himself, to get rid of his inhibitions once and for all and express his whole being unreservedly. He thought of the painter Paul Gauguin, who, in middle age, left his wife and children and took off for the South Seas. True, he died miserable, syphilitic and longing for France, but he left imperishable paintings. And Gauguin had done his own thing in his own way, fully expressing what was in him, whereas he, Ray Slingsby, had so far failed. If he did not act now he would die shrivelled and unfulfilled, forever regretting his timidity.

Ray, who had done some painting, over the years, also admired Gulley Jimson in Joyce Cary's novel *The Horse's Mouth*. Jimson was an artist who lived only for his art and its expression, caring little for material things. Such a life, thought Ray, was the highest form of life. An artist was so involved in the process of creation that he had no time for self-pity or thoughts of the futility of existence. Then, realising that he was being carried away by the drink, Ray brought his thoughts back to earth. He could not dignify this weekend as any sort of exercise in creative art, though if he was frank with himself, he hoped it might be an exercise in sex.

'Feeling all right, Ray?' Billy sounded concerned, but his real concern was whether Ray, who looked as if he had had more than enough to drink, would be capable of playing his due part when the time came. If he passed out on them now it would be a disaster.

Ray said that he was okay, though a bit tired, and gave Sarah a reassuring tap with his foot – a little investment perhaps in what was to come, and damn the lot of them. He was going to live before he died and stop being desiccated and dried-up. Defiantly, he took a large mouthful of his pudding – Death by Chocolate.

Billy drove back to the cottage slowly and

carefully but erratically. He only just avoided the trees, which he thought were moving out towards him, and he knew he was well over whatever limit they had in Ireland. They were bound to have some laws against drunken driving, and he was dimly aware that however hard he concentrated there were limits to the control that a brain drowned in alcohol could have over the movements of hands and feet. He didn't find it easy to judge distances, for example, and kept clipping the kerb on the near-side and once or twice on the off-side, which was asking for trouble. Fortunately the road was empty and when the others showed understandable concern he assured them that there would not be many Garda cars around in that country area. If they didn't b'leeve it, he said, slurring his words badly, they could get out and walk. Ray suggested he should go in front with a red flag, then Janet asked why not a red light, and everybody howled with merriment, though Ray laughed less than the others. He had seen the statements and photographs in many cases where drink and comedy had led to tragedy.

By a minor miracle they reached the cottage safely, and Billy dispensed brandy and Tia Maria as they sat in the front room with its low ceiling and a fire that – as they discovered when they lit it – smoked rather badly because of the birds' nests in the chimney. Ray and Sarah were sitting on the settee, while Janet sat on the floor, joined by Billy when he had handed round the drinks and put on a record: Frank Sinatra's 'My Way'. This was old hat, the women agreed, and it didn't suit Sarah at all, but Ray liked it.

The pair of them were getting on well together now, talking with quiet intimacy. Ray asked Sarah more about her work as a model, her training and how she got assignments. Sarah was flattered by Ray's interest; she was glad to be interrogated by this gentle caring man, though he didn't seem to be trying hard to get her into bed and she wished he would try a bit harder. It was great, being so close together in this time capsule, away from England, with no-one to know or care what they were doing. What a splendid idea Billy had had – it could be a terrific night.

Billy and Janet were already lying on the floor together, nuzzling, kissing and fondling. Sarah wondered how far they would go in public, and how far she and Ray would go. She seemed to have known him for ages, not hours. His soft gentle voice and manner, combined with his obvious strength as a person, in mind and body, had got through to her. She hoped for a move from him very soon.

Then Ray put his hand on hers, not dramatically but casually, as if he wasn't trying to send a signal or even concentrating on what he was doing. She turned her body a little towards his (as Janet, squinting with difficulty over Billy's head, was glad to see) so that her breast touched his arm. Ray liked that. It was obvious – as Sarah had intended it to be – that she was bra-less under her blouse, and he longed to put his hand there, to open the buttons one by one.

How long was it since he had touched a woman in that way, Ray wondered. Years and years. The only nubile female bodies he had looked at had been in the topless tabloids and magazines such as *Mayfair* and *Playboy*. He would never seek out hard porn such as he had seen in court – children and animals – but he had bought soft porn occasionally, reading it in secret. Helen would have derided him if she had known, telling him to grow up instead of behaving like a smutty schoolboy. So he kept the magazines hidden away in the drawer of his desk, in the study where he pored over briefs while still at the Bar and wrote judgements when on the bench.

He had not bought any magazines since he had become a judge, merely perusing the old ones from time to time. Tits and bums did not date, though it was not true – it could not be – that when you'd seen one pair you'd seen them all. Variety was an essential part of the game. Women knew what men thought about breasts, and that was why most women were so obsessed with the size and shape of their own. No woman was ever happy with them, as far as Ray could tell. They were always too big or too small or too droopy or had to be expensively packaged to make the most of them or even padded out with silicone implants.

Mr Justice Slingsby was still tempted to buy a magazine from time to time, but he always resisted. These days he might be recognised, followed and snapped, and the *Sun* would tell the world what an evil man he was, paying for porn, even though they peddled it themselves, making millions for Mr Murdoch.

Billy disentangled himself from Janet, refilled their glasses and put on a Shirley Bassey tape – 'I've got you under my skin.' This was old-hat too, but there were no tapes or records less than twenty years old in the cottage. Then Billy rejoined Janet on the floor, and Ray saw them get down to things in a more businesslike way. Billy kissed Janet warmly, openly and tonguily, then reached his hand round her back and tried to undo her bra, which he did not find easy as it fastened at the front. Realising his error, Janet undid it for him and removed it, exposing an ample, undulating pair of breasts, which Ray suspected had already been seen by better men than Billy.

The sight of Janet's breasts and Billy nuzzling and guzzling away at them had its effect on Ray, who found himself, reassuringly when he considered how much he had drunk, starting to rise to the occasion. His own cheek was touching Sarah's, which was warm and soft, and he kissed her lightly on it, then again, less lightly and for a fraction longer. Despite his radical views, he retained a lawyer's caution in some areas and this was one of them.

Then Sarah surprised but pleased him by quickly, impulsively turning to him and kissing his lips with her own warm, moist ones. She kept them closed, though. She too was playing it cool, he thought, though 'cool' was not the precise word he would have used in those circumstances. He drew back and they looked into each other's eyes and there was longing in both. He kissed again and this time her lips parted, as did his, and their tongues touched and flicked and teased as she explored his mouth and he responded. This was progress beyond all his expectations. There could be no withdrawal now, even if the *Sun* knocked on the door and called through the letter-box.

Several delicious minutes passed, but timing such events when you are part of them was difficult, Ray concluded, and looking at your watch could be misunderstood. Sarah opened the prospect of Heaven a little wider by taking Ray's left hand – how did she know he was left handed? he wondered wildly – and putting it on her right breast, which was slightly, very slightly larger than the left, though Sarah did not select it for that reason. Ray moved his hand over the warm moving mound, still encased in her thin blouse. 'Yes, yes,' she murmured as Ray touched the second button down. He hesitated for a moment in case she changed her mind, but 'Yes, yes,' she said again, so he fumbled with the button, trying to negotiate its path through the hole one-handed with fingers that felt strangely numb.

Ray could not know, but he soon became aware, that Sarah had abandoned her rules and her reticence. She did want this man, this gentle man, this gentleman judge. He would not let her down, and she trusted him. She wanted him now, to feel the hardness she had already detected, to feel it inside her. She wanted him to do with her what he wanted, with his strong firm hands, his strong firm will – and his strong firm prick.

Men of Ray's age could keep going for much longer than young bucks, once they got started, but meanwhile she must do her best to help him. It was becoming clear to her that she had far more experience than this man, even though he was older than her own father. It seemed that Ray would take hours just to undo one button, so she took his hand and guided it under her blouse and on to her nakedness, where it should have been minutes ago. He could hardly believe that he was in actual contact with the warm, firm moving flesh, the erect nipple, but he was, and after gently kneading and feeling Sarah's right breast he moved awkwardly on to the left – you had to treat both equally, and he could not be sure which one he preferred. In the end he settled for the right one, which was easier to reach and to manipulate.

'Yes, yes.' Protected by the Pill, Sarah wanted him to take her through the turbulent torrent, till the tip of his prick exploded within her and they came together as she hoped they would. They would go tumbling, turning, twisting, dreaming, dying, living, yearning, finding, losing, loving over the warm waterfall. Then into the calm quiet waters below and beyond, and on to the cool sand where they would lie silent and a little sad, but glad to be together, to recover and walk hand in hand for a while, then again and again and again. Sarah had had such desires before and they had never been fully realised. But this time they must.

'Yes, yes,' as Ray's hand reached slowly towards the seat of all rapture, the centre of life. He was drawn there as inevitably as eels are drawn to the Sargasso Sea, that calm area of the North Atlantic between the West Indies and the Azores where seaweed floats and eels wriggle their relentless way to their paradise as Ray was doing, or trying to do, towards his. Eels are unable to halt or divert, they are driven by desires they did not create, cannot control and must obey. And so it was for the Honourable Mr Justice Raymond Slingsby, whose judgement had been overtaken by the flood, and he knew there was no way they could stop now, though if Sarah had said 'Stop' he hoped he would be able to manage it. But he thought from the way she was behaving that the problem was unlikely to arise. His only nagging doubt was whether he could keep going long enough, because whatever happened he must not disappoint this trusting young goddess.

Ray's left hand touched the edge of the brief, oh so fantastically brief panties and hovered there as if unsure which route to take. He was very near the action now, the firing-line, and a mistake could be disastrous.

Mr Justice Slingsby decided to take the overland route, slowly running his fingers across the mound and causing gasps of pleasure and murmurs of pleasurable anticipation from its owner.

'Go on, Ray, please.'

He reached the ridge beyond, and slowly, gently explored it and its earthworks.

'Yes, Ray. Don't stop.' He was overcome by excitement, but in spite of all, his flag of sex was still only at half mast, which was potentially fatal to all his hopes for himself and promises to Sarah. How could he stiffen his resolve? Not by will, however much he gritted his teeth and urged himself on. There was some invisible primeval mechanism at work here that no-one understood. It did not happen to young men, who could rise again and again, and once more he mourned the opportunities that he had passed up through mistaken morality in years gone by.

The French were right. 'Si jeunesse savait, si vieillesse pouvait': if youth had the knowledge and old age the capacity! Sarah would not wait much longer, he thought to himself as he resumed his pilgrimage of what he still hoped would be pleasure, and his finger began its slow descent into the still covered cavern.

He should have been delighted, but instead he became alarmed when Sarah suddenly began to go wild. Her mouth, fully open and demanding, covered Ray's face with kisses. She was breathing deeply. 'Oh my God. Oh my God.' Her pelvis began to thrust against his hand, in desperate rhythmical thrusts. She tore at her panties, ripping them as she threw them aside desperately. Hastily she seized Ray's zip. Too hastily. She couldn't find the tag.

'Help me, Ray. Help me, please.' He found the tag and pulled it down a few centimetres, reluctantly, because he knew that the moment of truth was coming, and he would have to do what he was uncertain whether he could. Any moment now Sarah would know, if she did not know already, what the state of play was, or wasn't – and there would be no play that day, by the look and feel of things. What on earth was he going to do? How could he possibly explain? How could he expect this willing, thrilling, warm and ready young girl to understand and forgive? She tore at the tag of his zip, but it was stuck; it did that sometimes.

'Help me, Ray, oh do help. For Christ's sake!'

Janet Yorke suddenly jumped to her feet and pushed past them. 'Oh heavens. The loo!' She raced from the room.

Ray and Sarah paused. He was glad of the diversion, but she was not. What was going on? Sarah asked herself hazily. Why had Janet rushed away as if the house was on fire? How very selfish of her to interrupt at such a crucial moment.

She did not know that Janet had realised she was about to witness the very thing that she and Billy had planned and waited for, the event on which the whole venture turned. The act that they had hoped to record on film was about to take place there, downstairs, in front of them both, which was most convenient, but only if she had her camera ready. And she didn't – she had meant to slip it in her handbag before they went out for the evening, but had stupidly forgotten and left it in her case upstairs.

Hurling herself into the bedroom she tore into her bag, throwing out clothing and make-up until she unearthed the vital piece of equipment.

Panting, she paused for a moment to catch her breath and steady her hands. She was just about to launch herself downstairs again when she heard a thudding, splintering crack which stopped her dead in her tracks.

Ray, Billy and Sarah gaped in shock as the locked front door of the cottage burst open and four dark fit-looking young men in jeans and jerseys raced in. The leading one brandished a sledge-hammer threateningly at them; the others waved hand-guns.

'Down on the floor' and 'Don't move or you're dead' came the contradictory orders. 'Down, down, down.' The voices had thick Irish accents.

Sarah fell to the carpet at once, instinctively but unsuccessfully trying to replace her knickers and pull down her blouse at the same time – not an easy thing to do in any circumstances.

Ray, being older and less supple, took a moment or two longer to react, though he did his best. 'What's this? What's going on? Who are you?'

He did not seriously expect any answers but the questions showed that even the desperation of his plight had not undermined Raymond Slingsby's instinctive method of finding his way through any troublesome situation. The only reply to his interrogation, and one which he did not regard as satisfactory and in other circumstances would have said so, was, 'Don't move or you're dead.'

The three on the floor – for Billy had gone to ground without protesting or reacting in any obvious way – were frisked roughly by three pairs of hands as the sledge-hammer man held up his implement in a menacing way. The one who searched Sarah, who was lying on her back, lifted her blouse and she felt affronted and ashamed, though too terrified to say so.

'Well, well, well,' the man said, expressing his deep appreciation for her breasts, though in a very unimaginative way for an Irishman.

'Well, well, well,' he said again. He touched one breast with each hand, but not offensively – more like a doctor feeling for lumps – then allowed Sarah to pull down her blouse again. It seemed to Sarah that her breasts were drawing even more attention from the male sex than usual, but so far they had not been harmed, at least. If she survived – and she could not help fearing the worst – then her breasts had to survive too. Whatever would she do without them, she wondered as she lay there breathing heavily again, but not from sexual excitement. Meanwhile, the Irishmen continued their search, but no other weapons were uncovered.

Upstairs, Janet was listening to the noises and voices, her heart thumping violently. My God, she thought, it's the IRA. We're all going to be shot. Soon they would come upstairs and find her. Where could she hide? How could she escape?

The windows in the bedroom had not been opened for years and anyway the drop outside was too far for her to jump. But the bedroom had a recess on one side and in it was the jacketed hot-water cylinder. Pipes behind the cylinder led up through a hole in the low ceiling into the cold water tank in the roof-space.

Janet hastily threw all the clothes she could see into her case. She knew she had to take it with her otherwise they'd realise there'd been a fourth person in the cottage. Then she squeezed painfully round the cylinder. It was a tight fit, but she had to make it – her life depended upon it, she thought as she shoved and pushed – and by thrusting a section of the jacket aside, she did.

There wasn't that much space to climb up between the piping, and at first she thought she'd never succeed, but then she heard footsteps come up the stairs and go into the first bedroom. She *had* to do it, and in a last, desperate push she forced her shoulders between two pipes, grazing one arm and almost dropping her suitcase.

The footsteps went into the room next to hers. With strength she didn't know she had, she hauled herself on to the ledge where the water tank was. There was a small space behind it, and by forcing her head down at an unbearable angle she squeezed in there and held her breath, as the footsteps came into her room. The man had a torch and he shone it into the recess. If he found her would he shoot her for trying to escape, even though she had never been his captive? You couldn't expect the IRA to be logical. And no-one would hear the gun-shots in this isolated spot. The man withdrew the torch and she heard him rummaging around looking for her.

'Where the devil are you? You're here somewhere. You won't get away.'

The beam from the torch flickered back to the recess and he shone it up to the roof and on to the tank. If she moved or breathed now, she was dead.

'Fucking hell,' he said to himself. 'The bastard's gone.' And he stumped out of the room and down the stairs.

Was their mad, bad escapade going to end in tragedy, Janet asked herself, listening for the sound of gunfire from below. She should have known something like this would happen, she thought. Any plan cooked up by Billy was almost guaranteed to go wrong. Knowing that the other men might still come up and make a more thorough search, she did not dare move from her hiding place. Thank God they were Irish, because although she realised it didn't do to be racist, one had to admit that the Irish weren't always as thorough as, say, the Germans. Not that this was a criticism of the Irish. They were charming people even if they didn't get up at dawn to put their towels on the best sunbeds – or all those they'd met had been charming, but then they hadn't yet come face to face with the IRA, or had they?

Janet realised her thoughts were running away with her and tried to get a grip on herself. What a tale she would have to tell – and, indeed, sell – if she lived to recount this evening's events. She heard the sound of footsteps leaving the house and crunching across the gravel outside towards the lane. Silence followed, then a car, no two cars, started up some way off and drove away into the further distance. It was very quiet, very lonely. She wondered what to do next. Had they left a man at or near the cottage, silently waiting for her, a gun in his hand?

8

THE CARD on the door of the private room said 'His Honour Judge Alwyne Chandelle-Sweet QC'. As she went in to pay her early morning visit, Dr Roma Selinski wondered again if 'QC' was correct, but she wanted to be on the safe side. That was why she had ordered the judge a single room despite him being a National Health patient.

Dark, pretty twenty-seven-year-old Dr Selinski had several phobias in addition to those that all psychiatrists have. One was about going to court and being torn into tiny pieces in public by clever bewigged barristers and judges. This was more than a mere phobia – it had happened to her several times. She knew that her reports were long-winded and that she used long words. That was why they made fun of her.

She had tried to change her approach, but it was too late. The doctor had learnt her psychiatry at the Maudsley hospital in London under Dr Stefan Gattowski, and his example had convinced her that long-windedness was an essential requirement for any psychiatrist.

She was not hostile to courts and lawyers, only afraid of them. When able to think rationally about the subject, she knew that the courts tried to be good to doctors, putting on cases at times that were convenient for them on the basis, sometimes justified, that they were busy people with a queue of anguished patients awaiting their skill and patience.

Dr Selinski also realised that lawyers were not entirely disinterested in this concern for the medical profession. Every judge or barrister knew that one day he could be in an operating theatre, with the masked men and women standing over him, sharpening their knives. He would then, if the anaesthetic had not yet taken effect, say to himself, 'I hope they remember that I always tried to get their cases on first.' This accounted for the popularity of medico–legal societies, which were founded on love–hate born of mutual wariness.

Dr Selinski had once met Judge Chandelle-Sweet at a medico–legal society meeting where the subject had been 'The Legal Aspects of Sado-Masochism'. He had puzzled her then by some of the things he had said, when he appeared to confuse SM with MS and assume that the two conditions were related. And during her interviews with him over the two days since he had been brought to St Felix's Hospital following his unfortunate encounter with the press and the police, he had continued to puzzle her.

For example, he had been in doubt about his mother's forenames, although he said he had lived with her until he was twenty-two. Dr

Selinski had only come across this previously with schizophrenics, but she thought it unlikely that an English judge would be suffering from this condition. Amnesia could account for it, but as far as she could ascertain there was no history of that. And there were other worrying and inexplicable features in a case that was so interesting that she was thinking of writing it up for the *Journal of Psychiatry*, without identifying the patient.

The judge's account of how he came to be lying in his nightclothes, partially exposed, on top of a police sergeant in the presence of the national and international media, had baffling features. It so happened that Sergeant Spudding had also been referred to Dr Selinski by his superiors, once they had read the tabloids. She thought it unethical to have both men as her patients, so her colleague Dr Emil Singh had examined the sergeant, and the two accounts – she had considered it within ethical bounds to compare them, though it was a grey area – differed significantly.

The sergeant said that the judge had assaulted him, though he would not go so far as to allege indecent assault. The judge said that the sergeant got in the way by sheer carelessness while he, the judge, was doing no more than escape from harassment by the media, with which any ordinary decent citizen would surely sympathise. Dr Selinski had thought, naively, that two men trained in different aspects of law enforcement would agree on the main parts of their odd escapade, but the English never ceased to astonish her by their eccentricities, and of course it was these which made their country such fertile ground for psychiatrists.

Dr Selinski had come to Britain three years previously, to study under the great Dr Gattowski – they both came from Cracow university originally. Dr Gattowski had interpreted the words 'to study under' too literally. Dr Selinski had had enough of that in Poland and she had hoped that British doctors would be less sexually rapacious. She was wrong, but she drew the line at Dr Gattowski. He was too old, and had an itchy beard, and while brilliant at psychiatry was less than brilliant at sex, in fact nothing but a boor and a bore, or even a boar (she had been taking lessons from a teacher of English for foreigners, a nice young man).

Having gone through the rest of the judge's history, Dr Selinski felt that she had to ask him about the false degree allegation. The judge immediately complained of a blinding pain in the head, saying he could not remember any of the details of university life after twenty-five years. This confirmed the doctor's suspicion about amnesia caused by a head injury. She entered this in the notes and underlined it as a definitive finding.

She then told Alwyne she was keeping him in for observation for a further few days, and her patient was over the moon with excitement. He would not have to go to court in any capacity for the immediate future, and the media would not be able to get at him. He had already refused to read any newspapers, watch TV or listen to the radio, and had further insulated himself from reality by trying to read two Jeffrey Archer novels.

Before leaving, Dr Selinski told Alwyne that he could have a light breakfast. Whether she meant by this burnt unbuttered toast and unsweetened tea, he had no means of discovering, but that is what he got. He was, after all, an NHS and not a private patient. He decided to add to that not very generous repast the black grapes his darling wife Anona had sent in, being too busy with her daily duties to come herself. But the grapes had been going off when they arrived and were now completely rotten.

In spite of the deficiencies of the catering, Judge Chandelle-Sweet felt that it was worth feigning madness, which was easier than he knew, so as to be kept in hospital for a longer period. In a week or two, everything would die down, and a war in the Middle East, or an economists' battle nearer home, would divert the media and he could quietly resume his judicial career. It was a pity he had never managed to finish the biscuit case, but he could release it to another judge who would have to start it again. It couldn't be helped, and at least he wouldn't have to make a fool of himself by asking how that biscuit got into the plaintiff's mouth. Although he would still quite like to know.

Alwyne, feeling much better, opened Archer's *First Among Equals* again and determined he would get beyond page 102. His health was improving, but whatever else he must not demonstrate that to anyone. The iller he looked, the better, he must remember. He put down the book and placed his head under the bedclothes, symbolising his attitude to the world, should the world be interested.

Lord Chancellor Trotter had got into bed a few minutes earlier that same morning. He was feeling pleased in a tentative way and feeling his private secretary in a routine, almost casual, way. He was certain, he tried to reassure himself, that things were going to turn out all right. That the brilliantly conceived plan to discredit Slingsby had even now been put into action by Billy Wickstead-Hacking and his friends. But to be as frank with himself as he would never be with others, Trot could not help suspecting that Billy was capable of making a monumental cock-up. No, he must not think like that. He must have confidence in Billy and also in himself. It had been a desperate situation calling for bold measures which must and would succeed.

Even though it was still early, he could not help feeling slightly disappointed that he had heard nothing from Ireland. Billy had arranged that when he had acquired the incriminating evidence he would send one cryptic word 'GOTCHA'. But how was he going to send it? They had not gone into that. Telegrams had been abolished, hadn't they? He wasn't sure, but at times like these how could you be sure of anything? If Billy phoned and said, 'This is Wickstead-Hacking. Tell the Lord Chancellor – "Gotcha",' what would they think in the office downstairs?

It might sound like a threat. Would they call in

the Special Branch, and what would they uncover? He couldn't expect the Prime Minister to support him: there was no loyalty among politicians. The one-word message was Kingston's idea, but you couldn't expect an idiot who got a double first in Classics to have any common-sense. He'd have Kingston transferred to the Ministry for Recreation when all this was over. Then he'd be able to bore everybody with how many runs he made in the 'Varsity match, if he did make any.

He must keep control and keep calm for the next few hours, Trot told himself. He was a great man in a great office of state, and no-one had as much power and influence, not even Saddam Hussein. He was Oswald Trentham Hurlingham, first Viscount Trotter of St Pancras, though he had long ago quietly turfed out the Hurlingham. It was too easy for nasty malicious people like Raymond Slingsby to make jesting references to it. How he loathed that man. Of all the people in the great profession of the law, adorned at the top by his humble self, Slingsby – slinking, stinking, Raymond Slingsby – was the worst. Such socialist bastards had no place on the High Court bench or any other bench where responsible people sat in judgement. Men like that had to be run out of public life, pilloried, held up to ridicule and – this was the crux of the matter and the cross on which Slingsby would be crucified – they had to be solemnly voted out of office by both Houses of Parliament.

What better evidence could there possibly be of

judicial debauchery that would justify this than photographs of him actually on the job? But the photos had better be clear, beyond question, or Billy Bunter had better watch out. He would not get his judgeship, ever, if he botched things. No, he must think positively. The message should be coming through at any moment – saying that at last Slingsby had got his come-uppance. It could be downstairs already, waiting for the staff to arrive at nine o'clock or whenever they did arrive. Probably nearer quarter-past or even half-past, he thought, as they doubtless took advantage of the fact that he didn't go downstairs till later.

Nonie had her back to him, and yes, she had actually fallen asleep while he'd been day-dreaming. He put his arm round her back and touched her more than ample left tit. She did not move. She had the nerve to nod off at this moment of crisis, when every member of the staff should feel privileged and eager for work, even though it was a Saturday. But he couldn't trust any of them. They were all letting him down, and they'd know about it when the Slingsby thing was over and the sun shone once more.

Trot touched her again, aiming for the right tit, but he couldn't reach it. The left one would block his path until she turned to face him and to do her duty. An awful thought struck the Lord Chancellor – that his private secretary had stopped breathing. She was very still, but warm, and dead people were cold – though not immediately. Suppose she'd had a heart attack or a stroke, how would he know? He hadn't a clue.

One couldn't be an expert in every field. She was breathing, but why wouldn't she wake up? He pushed her left buttock and it trembled. That would be the fat, an automatic reaction from all that tissue when suddenly stimulated. Another push, a heavier one, and Nonie moaned. Thank the Lord for that. If she gave up the ghost at this delicate stage everything would be ruined. How do you dress a dead body of that shape and size? He'd never manhandle her on his own, and he couldn't ring for Kingston or that double-barrelled frosty-faced lesbian.

What could he tell them that would sound plausible? That Mrs Chandelle-Sweet had arrived early that Saturday morning to see to urgent personal letters and his car expenses, and had suddenly had hysterics, taken off all her clothes and dropped dead? He had a way with words when on form, and had swayed many a jury into letting off obviously guilty people, and a few into convicting obviously innocent ones, but the advocacy that would be required if Nonie did drop dead would strain the talents of a George Carman, Gilbert Gray and Quintin Hailsham rolled into one – and what a one they would make.

He mustn't let his thoughts meander, yet you had to be prepared. If Nonie did get seriously ill, what would be the best thing? She moaned again, a longer deeper moan. Could he say that she'd had a sudden fit and collapsed and he'd given her the kiss of life, she'd come round quickly, misinterpreted his gesture, taken off all her clothes before he could stop her, and collapsed again? His juries had swallowed more absurd tales. And nobody would cross-examine him about it. The staff were terrified of him. No, that was too strong – respectful, properly. They never questioned anything he said or did – or if they did question him he would have them transferred immediately and they knew that. The same applied to the police who looked after him, though most were splendid fellows.

There was the time he had been driving his Bentley Mulsanne back from Lord Hailsham's farewell party in the absence of Fred, his wretched chauffeur, who'd been selfish enough to go to Cyprus on holiday. When the Bentley touched the lamp-post – actually it knocked it over, but then Bentleys were heavy cars – the officer came up very high and mighty, but he soon changed his tune when he knew who he was talking to, and even joked about it. 'That lamp-post didn't ought to have come out and hit your Lordship's car like that, sir. It didn't know you as well as I know you, your Lordship.'

And the understanding officer had straightened out the front wing – not easy for him, that – and even driven the Bentley to Trot's home when the AA didn't come. They were always helping somebody else when you needed them, the wretched people. What a very pleasant policeman he was – our police really were wonderful. That one, what was his name – did he say 'Call me Bob, sir'? Or was it Bill? He'd chatted so respectfully as he drove out to Staines, and there wasn't a mention of the breathalyser, which he'd had in his hand when he came up in the street. It was a great night, that, and he'd always be grateful to PC Bill or Bob for not spoiling it.

Nonie sneezed three times. So all was well. Dead people didn't sneeze and dying ones probably didn't. Sneezing was a luxury confined to healthy living people. She hadn't been fully awake all the time and pretending, had she?

'Nonie!'

Anona stirred slightly. 'Ugh?'

'Nonie, listen to me.'

She opened her eyes a fraction. 'What is it? What do you want?'

'You haven't been listening to my thoughts, have you?'

'What a bloody stupid thing to say. Even for you, Trot, that's the bloody stupidest thing you ever said.'

To be honest with himself, as Trot occasionally managed to be, it wasn't a very sensible remark, but there was no need for Nonie to be so rude. That's what came of treating people too well. You had to keep your distance, or there was a danger they'd become too familiar, and that's what had happened with her, sadly. She had her good points; he touched the left one again and tried to steer her round to face him.

'Ow! Get off my boob, you great fat pudding.'

He *had* been too familiar with her, and it didn't pay. He'd be more careful with her replacement, and the sooner she came the better; he'd had enough of this one. But meanwhile he felt like a fuck, and there was no-one else immediately available. Everything was going off in this once great country. When he was young there'd been no difficulty in finding suitable women. But now . . .

He looked at Nonie's nakedness and he did not like it. There were dark patches under both her eyes, as if someone had punched her. It certainly wasn't him, though he had often felt like it recently. That husband of hers, his Honour Judge Alwyne Chandelle-Sweet, as he was now so proud to call himself – he couldn't have punched her, because she'd only have to sit on him and he'd be knackered.

What a jumped-up little jerk that Chandelle chap was. According to the press cuttings which came in weekly from an agency, he had addressed solicitors at his local law society and said 'Don't think of me as a judge, but as a barrister who has achieved high distinction through hard work and merit.' What confounded bloody impertinence!

Nonie's face was puffier than it used to be, and so were her great breasts. They used to be so exciting, those proud protuberances, so firm, unyielding even as she had yielded avidly, unreservedly, enjoying every touch. He had liked them best when she lay on him and let them hang deliciously while he took them in his hungry mouth like big ripe grapes, full of the juice of life. He had never seen such magnificent tits, and he'd seen a lot. But Nonie's appendages were not what they had been, and that was the snag with large ones, they did go off, go down rather, as the pull of gravity took over.

Trot looked at Nonie again. Even so, there was

207

still something to be said for that body, so he took her hand in his and placed it on his prick. Fucking was fucking, whoever it was, provided she was fuckable.

The phone rang while Trotter was inside and on the final straight, so they ignored it. It rang again, but he still hadn't made it. Eventually he did, to his relief, and hers. A moment later they were both shocked, by loud, urgent and repeated knocking on the door to the flat.

Lord Trotter was furious – it must be *her* again. She had no right, he said to himself. They had a clear agreement and he had been very fair. Throwing on his dressing-gown, he went to the door of the flat, bracing himself for the worst.

It was not his wife, but his permanent secretary. 'Lord Chancellor. Lord Chancellor. It's very urgent!'

'What is it, Kingston? I'm busy.'

'So sorry to interrupt you, Lord Chancellor.' Please come down at once. There's a *very* urgent message from Ireland.'

Shortly after 10 a.m., in a small room at Skibbereen's old Garda station, Mr Justice Raymond Slingsby was feeling both old and small, despite being nearly six feet tall and only fifty-one. Across a bare table he faced Detective Chief Superintendent Herman Patrick O'Flynn, a large fat man with a puffy round face who looked tired and was, having been aroused from his bed at 5.10 a.m. and driven to Skibbereen from Clonakilty at the abnormal and normally illegal speed of 75 m.p.h.

He had been told that the mission was urgent and that the fate of a British minister or maybe their whole government could depend on it. There could also be repercussions in Dublin, the Minister of Justice had explained on the phone. The Chief Super had never had an inquiry as important-sounding as this. Part of his work was taken up with looking for alleged terrorists – some were his personal friends, so it could be embarrassing – as well as the usual burglaries and motoring cases. He thought it more important to catch speeding motorists than burglars – it was easier, and speeding endangered everybody, while burglars mainly menaced the wealthy, who could afford it and anyway made a profit by filling in insurance claim forms more generously towards themselves than the facts warranted.

Herman O'Flynn had a confused attitude to the Brits as a race. His father christened him Herman because of his admiration for Hermann Goering; the Patrick had to be added because the Church insisted that at least one christian name was a saint's, and even his anti-British father doubted whether Goering would qualify.

The Brits were an odd lot, Herman Patrick had often told his fellow pool players as they drank the night away till his wife rang and threatened to report him to a TD (Irish for MP). The TD in question was her father, so Herman usually complied. The Brits were okay when Herman took his lads to visit the Met. in London on courses. They were hospitable though too sober, which surprised him at first as young Brit football supporters were known to be world champions in the alcoholics games.

On the other hand – and this is what had got to his dad – the Brits of 1919–22 had sent their Black-and-Tan soldiers to murder and torture patriotic Irishmen – patriotic towards their own country whereas the Brits expected Irishmen to be patriotic towards a foreign country. They even arrested his grandmother Roisin O'Flynn, and she got five ears, till a kind Welsh police inspector looked the other way and let her go. So it was a bit of a muddle when you tried to weigh up the Brits.

Their politicians were as stupid as any could be, that was Herman's opinion, but all politicians in any country including Ireland were only after Number One. On the other hand Margaret Thatcher had not only been a politician but a woman, which made it worse, and she had no sense of humour which made it much, much worse. In the present inquiry he must not be influenced by political considerations, but do his duty – using his discretion – and question this judge like any suspect in any type of case, speeding for instance.

He had no fellow officer with him. There hadn't been time, and he hadn't bothered – they gossiped about their cases, and that wouldn't do with this one. In one way some assistance would have come in useful, though. He had been out with the lads till 1.30 a.m., playing pool for the Skibbereen force against the Limerick lads, and it was no joke playing against Limerick, it wasn't funny at all.

They cheated by holding back and letting Skibbereen do all the drinking, and it wasn't fair on his own team, they were a good bunch and he was very proud of them – there wasn't a teetotaller among them. There had been one who got in the team last year, but when they sussed him out he'd been dropped as a disruptive influence, and the Chief soon transferred him to Limerick.

'Mr, er, Sir Slingsby,' Herman began, unsure quite how one was supposed to address a British judge.

'Raymond,' said Slingsby, letting him off the hook.

'That's very civil of you, sir. Call me Herman. Now. I have some notes here, and statements, but I've forgotten my glasses, and parts I can't make out, so I can't read them too easy like.'

'Could that be because you're holding them upside down?' Slingsby suggested diffidently.

Herman turned the papers round and peered at them again through bleary eyes. 'Ah, yes I am, so I am. That's very helpful of you, sir. Now you say you're a High Court judge in England.'

'Haven't you checked with London?'

'Oh yes, indeed we have. And there *is* a High Court judge by the name Raymond Percival Balderton Slingsby.'

'I dropped the Percival Balderton.'

'I can understand that, judge,' said Herman in a sympathetic way.

'You don't have my fingerprints, so you can't verify my identity, I suppose.' Rough as he felt, Slingsby still had his wits about him.

'That's quick, sir. You're ahead of me, as I'd expect from the English judiciary.'

'You've had personal experience of us?'

'My grandmother did have.'

'Oh, good.'

'To be honest with you, sir, it wasn't all that good. But it was a long time ago. Some things are best forgotten. Now, where was I? Bless me, but I've forgotten.' Herman leafed through his papers again, to no avail. Slingsby decided to help him out.

'Were you about to question me as to my arrest last night at the cottage?'

'I shall not be forgetting that. But I appreciate your assistance.'

Ray liked his interrogator. He wasn't the most efficient one he had ever encountered, but he had great charm. He wondered if his own forebears had been as delightful and unspoilt as the Irish before our Industrial Revolution swept honest toilers from their cottages into gaunt mills where owners and managers exploited them and their products, so that the owners grew rich and some of the kids never grew up at all.

Ray had been deeply shocked and – after it had become clear that he and his companions weren't being attacked by the IRA – embarrassed when the four members of the Irish Special Branch crashed their way into the cottage, thinking these odd English people were up to something nasty. It was Billy's evasiveness about what they were doing in Ireland, and his rambling on about bombs in the restaurant, that had got them into trouble. Yet how could the Garda have thought that the four were terrorists or any other sort of serious wrongdoers? Would such people wander around pubs dropping obvious clues? It seemed unlikely.

But now, Ray knew, innocent of any crime though he was, he was for the high jump and the long jump combined. He and Billy had only been bent on fun, and the criminal law did not come into it, though the church law might, but they already knew in London about his arrest, and they would tell the media – Trot would see to that.

Ray had played right into that man's hands, as he knew he ought to have anticipated. He felt sorry for Sarah; she wouldn't have as much to face back in England, but she'd be grilled – questioned, anyway – by the Garda. So would Billy, whose true role in all this, in the cold, sober light of morning, Ray couldn't help questioning. Billy was always one for a good time and bad women, but why the sudden desire to take Ray to Ireland, and his unusual – to be more accurate, unheard of – willingness to take on the expenses of the trip? Billy's qualities were many and varied, but they had never included generosity.

'Don't think I'm being too personal, Judge. I wouldn't want to do that, I can assure you. We've got some – how shall I say? – some interesting judges here. We have to look after them very, very closely and all that, and I know some of them very well indeed, I can tell you. A fine bunch of men. And they know how to enjoy themselves, most of them. But what I mean, sir, is this. I don't think I can imagine any of them getting mixed up with a Page Three girl, if you understand my meaning.'

Ray stared at Herman O'Flynn. 'What do you mean?'

'Surely you knew, sir. That young lady you were with last night – and very lovely she is too, I'm not saying that I blame you at all – tells us that she appears on page three of your fine British newspapers, and we know what *that* means, being men of the world. Now I couldn't believe one of our judges here would be caught spending the night with a girl like her, though I wouldn't know what they'll be doing when they go over!' Irish people called Britain 'over'.

Ray began to realise the full magnitude of his folly. Billy had told him that Sarah was a model, but he had understood this to mean that she was a fashion model, and Sarah herself had said nothing to contradict this in their conversations about her work. If she really was a Page Three girl, what a monumental idiot he had been. It was bad enough being caught sneaking off to Ireland with any girl, but with one who had been baring her tits in the tabloids for millions of men to lust after – the implications hardly bore thinking about.

It was bad enough now, having to admit he'd done something that not even an Irish judge was known to have done. The Chief Super must think he was a real disgrace, though he wasn't showing it. Ray wondered for a moment if he could somehow talk his way out of his predicament, but he realised that the only course to take was to tell the truth. The others would be interviewed separately, including Janet when they caught her, so there was no point in trying to be clever. He wondered about Janet. Was her presence on the trip really as innocent as she had claimed? And was it coincidence that she had been out of the room at the very moment the raid took place?

'Chief Superintendent, I must be frank with you. I am a married man and I came to Ireland hoping to have sex with that unfortunate young lady, and I have no excuse whatever, save to remind you that we were consenting adults in private.'

Herman was bowled over! Didn't consenting adults apply to acts of a disgusting nature between men? He knew the law was different 'over', but the judge wasn't saying the Page Three girl was a man? It could soon be checked, though not by him personally. But he had never come across this in all his twenty-seven years' service. A suspect – and the judge had to be so regarded – was making admissions of things that hadn't even been put to him! Nobody sane ever did that, not in Ireland. In his own interest the judge had to be told not to open his mouth before they opened it for him. Then Herman remembered with alarm that his omission could be fatal in any legal proceedings.

'Judge, I've forgotten to caution you.'

'That's very frank.'

'I was thinking the same about you.'

'Full disclosure, eh, Mr O'Flynn? It's a *uberrimae fidei* situation.' Then Ray wished he hadn't put it that way, and so did his interrogator.

'Pardon me, sir, but at school we didn't do Greek.'

'Latin, actually. We lawyers, we still talk Latin half the time,' said Ray apologetically.

'Same with us Guards, judge.'

That didn't seem likely, but he pressed on regardless. 'I'll regard myself as cautioned, Chief Superintendent.'

This pleased Herman, who always read the caution from a card in his pocket-book, and he had left it in his other suit. He liked this judge: a good sort. 'Look, sir, I see it like this. There's no need for confirmation from London. I accept you're a High Court judge – you've behaved like one.'

Ray didn't know how to take that.

'And if I may say so, judge, you're very welcome in this country. I wish we had more people like you here from over.'

How was Ray to take *that*? Were they short of womanisers?

'We can regard this little matter as closed, I think I can say that, judge. I'll have to put in my report to the Minister of Justice, but he's an understanding man – a man very much like yourself.'

'Oh, good,' Ray said. He wasn't sure what this meant, but he was still feeling so shell-shocked by the disclosure about Sarah that he really didn't care.

'And I shall – how shall we say? – I'll make sure my report puts things in the best way for you, by missing out some of the important parts.'

Ray felt the conversation was taking a strange turn, but there was more.

'We're not living in the twenty-first century for nothing, judge, not here in Ireland we're not. We're much more broad-minded now – but not as much as you people over. There's only one way to conclude this, if I may make a suggestion, sir, and that's over a pint or two of our best draught Guinness at the Robert Emmet across the road. It's on us, of course, seeing you've honoured us with your presence. It's been a boring few months we've had here, but you've livened things up, yes indeed you have, you and your friends.'

Ray groaned inwardly at the thought of more drink, but he knew there was no escape. 'Let me treat you, Chief Superintendent.'

'Ah, no, that could be misinterpreted. There are some very suspicious people around these days. The newspapers for one.'

Ray nodded agreement, wincing as he thought about his return to the UK.

'We have a special fund for occasions like this. As a matter of fact it's for the pool team, but if we don't tell them, they won't know, will they, judge?'

9

'WE'VE GOT him now, Kingston, fair and square, bang to rights, caught like a rat in a trap, eh?' Lord Chancellor Trotter was ecstatic. The telephoned report from the Minister of Justice in Dublin told of arrests during an orgy and of the judge and the Page Three girl being found in compromising circumstances.

'The filthy bastard. That's the sort of man he is, I always knew. He goes over there defying my ban, with a tart, and he's on the job in the same room as two other people when he gets arrested. What could be worse?'

'Murder?' said the permanent secretary.

'Don't be daft, Kingston.'

'It was part of the plan, to compromise him, was it not?' asked Sir Anthony, unimpressed by his master's hypocritical ranting. 'When Billy Wickstead-Hacking came here . . .'

'Because he wanted to be a judge,' snapped Trot, 'so I had to see him. But I don't know about any plan, and you don't either, if you know what's good for you.'

'Quite so, Lord Chancellor.'

'The sooner this disgusting business is over, the better for everybody – the judges, the public, they've all had this wretched Raymond Slingsby on their backs.'

'And Slingsby's campaign against you will be over too.' Sir Anthony could not help mentioning this tiny fact.

The Lord Chancellor put on his gravest official manner. 'We mustn't think of ourselves, Kingston. Duty comes first, and it's a painful duty, but it has to be done. The whole appalling episode – well, the key points of it – will have to be reported to Parliament. I shall not be at all surprised if both Houses decide to petition for Slingsby's dismissal. A very rare occasion, happily.'

'Never before in England. It has happened in Ireland.'

What a know-all Kingston was, thought Trot. 'All sorts of things go on in Ireland, Kingston, as we are well aware, and as Slingsby is now aware too.'

'Lord Chancellor, I must point out that Mr Justice Slingsby is likely to defend himself before Parliament.'

'He had a big practice, I realise that. Good at cross-examination. Eloquent at times. But, my God, he'll need all that and a hell of lot more to get himself out of a tangle like this – and one entirely of his own making.'

Kingston raised one eyebrow a fraction.

'All right, most of it, then,' Trot admitted reluctantly. 'You'd better go and look up the procedure, so I can inform the House.'

'There isn't any procedure, sir.'

Trot was annoyed. 'Then go and make one up. There has to be a proper procedure. Justice must be seen to be done, even to a judge. So go and get your thinking cap on, eh, Kingston – if you can find it.'

The civil servant did not look convinced. 'One last query, Lord Chancellor, if I may. The press – when are they to be informed?'

'Not yet. They'll hear about all this when I announce it in the House on Monday.'

After an unavoidable pint of Guinness, Ray Slingsby was driven in a Garda car to Cork airport. Billy and Sarah were to be released later that day. They weren't VIPs and had to wait for the wheels of Irish bureaucracy to grind.

As Ray's car drove through Bandon, TV presenter Janet Yorke was entering the *Courier* building in London. She felt recovered from her ordeal which, after the initial panic, had been less stressful than she might have predicted. There had been no-one about when she climbed down from the cottage's roof-space after a quiet and uncomfortable half-hour, and the hire-car was still in front of the house with the keys in the ignition. That struck her as odd: wouldn't the IRA have taken the car or set fire to it? Or had they accepted that there was no fourth person?

At first she intended to contact the police, but then she decided it wouldn't do any good. The Irish police botched things up, letting terrorists escape from hostage situations and forgetting to mark ransom money. They were like policemen in an old black-and-white Ealing comedy. It was tough on her three companions, but at times like this it was everyone for themselves. Her duty was to tell the public what had been going on.

She knew that the quickest way to do it was to telephone her TV station, but she was still determined to make some money out of this and it was the tabloids who paid best. So she drove to Cork airport, planning to take the first plane for London. While waiting for her flight, her conscience got the better of her. If the other three *had* been kidnapped by the IRA, she couldn't leave the country without at least making an attempt to inform the police.

She left it to the last possible moment before making her call to the Garda.

'Three English people kidnapped near Rosscarberry did you say? And one of them a High Court judge?' The voice answering the telephone seemed strangely untroubled by the news, thought Janet. 'Now isn't that a coincidence because we have three people answering your description safe and sound with the Garda at Skibbereen. And I think we can safely say that the IRA had nothing to do with it. Now, where did you say you were calling from, miss?'

Janet slammed down the phone and ran for her plane, praying that the call would not be traced before she was safely in the air. As she downed a large gin-and-tonic – it was very early but she had to have something to steady her nerves – she thought about what she had been told. If it hadn't been the IRA who burst into the cottage, then it must have been the police, thinking that *they* were potential terrorists. How absolutely ridiculous – but how perfect for her story.

The editor of the *Courier* was Bob Bamford, a fifty-two-year-old Scot who looked like a burly farmer and had shouted, sworn and sulked his way from a Glasgow slum to the tabloid slum that was the *Courier*. He stamped about the large open-plan floor where the journalists worked at their screens while he was there, and gossiped about him when he was not. No-one liked him except the news editor Colin McHeath who was as crude and rude as he was and owed his job to his fellow Glaswegian.

Although he had wide experience as a journalist, starting on a local paper in Scotland at sixteen, Bob Bamford was not good with words except for swear-words. When writing for the paper he used words as an unskilled labourer builds a wall with varying shapes of stones: he threw them in and hoped they would fit, and if they didn't the sub-editors did it for him.

He had however made a real contribution to the world of newspapers, as the *Courier*'s proprietor, small swarthy forty-seven-year-old Sir Malcolm Windsor, recognised. Bob Bamford recognised shit when he saw it and knew how to serve it to the British public – whose virtues were extolled in every leading article – and he knew how to make shit tasty. His chief aim in life after he became editor was 'to outgun the *Sun*', which sounded sense except to those who thought about it, which did not include the *Courier*'s 2.8 million purchasers and an estimated 8.1 million readers.

Janet put her cards on the editor's table as he welcomed her. His jacket was off as usual and he was wearing a white shirt with broad purple stripes. Bob listened to her story with glistening eyes and itching fingers. A High Court judge, the notorious Mr Justice Slingsby, caught at an orgy with a Page Three girl, about to bonk her when arrested by the 'IRA' who turn out to be policemen. And Janet Yorke as an eye-witness!

It was a tragedy that she hadn't taken pictures. That would have added up to a lot of money. Even so Bob could see the splash now: BONKING FROM THE BENCH, or HIGH CAUGHT ORGY. A leader would condemn such shocking misbehaviour by a man who had the nerve to lecture the Lord Chancellor. Judges should set an example. Slingsby must be slung out NOW. It was a pity the Page Three girl was over sixteen, or the judge could have been put in the real dock, and the story would have been worth even more. How much did Janet want for it as it stood?

Janet took a deep breath. 'A hundred grand.'

'Phew! No way.' The editor mopped his bald head with his handkerchief.

Janet stood up and turned towards the door.

'No, sit down a moment. Have you written out a statement I could have a look at?'

Janet was not falling for that. She would give no further details until a contract was drawn up by solicitors and signed. She wanted fifty grand on signing and then they could have her detailed story. The balance was to be paid the day after publication. Bamford asked for an option for twenty-four hours, which Janet refused. He could have one for four hours, she told him, for one grand paid in notes there and then.

Bob leaned back in his chair and removed his half-moons. 'A hundred grand's an awful lot of money. I've never paid anything like that, even for a bloody good story.'

Janet smiled. 'But you've never had a story like this before.'

This was true, but Bob Bamford had got his fingers burnt recently when he had paid twenty grand in notes as part payment for an eighty-grand story by a 'Royal dog-handler' about the goings on between a duchess close to the Throne and a dog that got too close to her. Bob had been excited about the story, which was both sensational and novel. 'Novel' had turned out to be truer than he knew. The 'dog-handler' had been nothing of the kind, but an unemployed deck-chair attendant who was scared of guard-dogs, had never been near a duchess and had a string of convictions for fraud. These facts came to light just in time for the front page to be pulled, and mercifully the other tabloids never found out about it, but Sir Malcolm Windsor did, and the loss of the £20,000 nearly killed him – he'd rather have lost his mother, he said.

Mindful that Sir Malcolm was not only his boss but a ruthless megalomaniac, Bob though it wise to consult him about the rest of the Janet deal. He

224

arranged an immediate payment in cash of the thousand pounds to her and she hurried away, saying that she had a phone-call to make and a plane to catch.

The *Courier*'s proprietor was born in Tel Aviv and had lived there till the age of fifteen as Moshe Weinstein. He then came to England to live with his Uncle Ben, who ran a local paper in Lancashire, but Malcolm Windsor, as the lad had become, soon graduated to a free newspaper circulating in North London. He told his friends his new name was easier to pronounce and spell than the old one, saying that if Windsor was good enough for the Queen it was good enough for him. He was a great patriot, and after he bought the *Courier* the Union Jack appeared everywhere: on the front page, on his notepaper, the walls of the six loos at Windsor Grange and on the driver's and front passenger doors of his Bentley Turbo R.

Windsor saw the possibilities of Janet's story immediately: 'Just the job to knock the *Sun* out of the ring.'

Bob doubted if it would do that, but he did not say so, as his proprietor sacked people who disagreed with him. Malcolm then asked Bob if Janet could be beaten down on price. Bob said no. Sir Malcolm told Bob to hold everything for two hours. He'd just had an idea, and would have to see someone higher up about it. Bob wondered who that could be, because surely the only person above Malcolm Windsor was the Lord himself. He did not know how close that was, as Malcolm rushed out, shouting instructions for his chauffeur.

Ray Slingsby was still sitting in the departure lounge of Cork airport three and a quarter hours after the departure time for his flight to North Midlands. An announcement in Irish that few understood would be followed by one in English that nobody understood: 'Due to operational reasons the departure of Flight EI928 to North Midlands is delayed by an hour,' and so on.

No-one went to ask what 'operational reasons' meant. Ray thought that the Irish and British were at odds about various matters, but united in their acceptance of being buggered about by officials without complaint or query. Operational reasons could mean the engines had become detached; that the pilot had suddenly decided he didn't like flying; that the aircraft had through computer-error been sent to a place called Cork in the Australian outback; or that an air stewardess had fallen for the co-pilot before take-off and locked herself in the loo till he agreed to marry her.

The possibilities were endless, but it was pointless for anyone to inquire because it wouldn't make any difference, they'd have to wait just the same, as helpless to improve their lot as dogs at a delayed feeding-time.

Ray was sipping his third Jameson's whisky and Canada Dry, staring into nothingness, when suddenly his eyes focused and his brain clicked into action. The man and woman who had just come in to the departure lounge were Billy

Wickstead-Hacking and Sarah Garrowby.

He got up and went over to them. 'So they let you go at last.' It was a statement of the obvious rather than a question. 'Did they give you any trouble?'

'Only by forcing Guinness down us,' said Sarah. She laughed, attempting to disguise the fact that for some reason she found this meeting embarrassing. 'I hope it won't make me fat.'

Ray looked at her and couldn't see any difference. She was still as nubile as she had been the night before. Those tits had blown him to bits, he thought, or would do soon. His marriage, job and reputation would all be shot to pieces because of his weakness for those delicious appendages.

Predictable as ever, Billy went off to buy a round of drinks, thinking that it was the least he could do. Things may not have gone according to plan, but he'd still caused Ray a lot of trouble.

There had been a noticeable downturn in Billy's mood while they were at the police station, and he saw everything more clearly now, but he couldn't see that Volvo 850GLT and he didn't think he ever would. As for a judgeship, he knew he could forget it. Everything had come apart and he'd been left holding the ashes: a defective metaphor, but it was expressed his present condition precisely. As did 'Looking at life through a window of tears'.

He felt overcome by self-pity, which he knew was wrong but that didn't dispel it. The next three months would be hell, but only his psychiatrist and a few friends would know the reason why.

That's what Billy thought, anyway, not appreciating that doctors were no more discreet about their cases than lawyers, and that everyone connected with medicine or the law on the North Midland Circuit knew he was a nut-case.

He would have to endure the next three months as best he could: the descent into darkness; no energy, not wanting to do anything, even to get out of bed. He had got through it all before, time after time, but every time it was worse and he wondered where it would end. As for the tablets, they did no good at all. Drink was better, but worse. He smiled at a thought that was absurd but true.

Sarah went to the ladies' to repair her make-up. She must look good, because at any time, according to Billy, the media might leap out and flash their cameras at them. She was hoping they would, so she'd be on page one instead of Page Three, which was definitely promotion. Billy had said there was no such thing as bad publicity, and the more notorious you became the more you got paid for your story. This could be her big break.

Things looked like turning out okay, she thought. Someone else could write her story and she'd get most of the cash and all the publicity. It was a pity about the judge. She'd liked Ray and they could have had a fantastic couple of days; he was a bit nervous but she could have cured him of that. That was life, though. You never knew what was going to happen next, but so long as men wanted you and you didn't throw yourself about so freely that they stopped wanting you, and you stopped respecting yourself, everything would be all right.

Yes, she liked Ray yet she couldn't feel really sorry for him. He was old enough to know what was what and he shouldn't be playing around with young women. It would be interesting to see what happened to him now. He looked worried as hell, but they couldn't put him in prison or cut his head off, or his hand or anything like that. What was he expecting that was going to be so awful?

As he followed Sarah and Billy out of the aircraft at North Midlands airport, Ray paused at the top of the steps and looked around. No press in sight, not a notebook or a camera, but then the media would not be allowed beyond the barrier he'd have to go through. After he'd passed through the green channel he'd see the red-eyed vultures, ready to pounce.

He must stay cool, he thought, as he walked slowly down the aircraft steps. He must be polite but say nothing at all. He'd asked Chief Superintendent O'Flynn if he could get North Midlands airport to let him through specially, but the reply had been that if they did if for judges they'd have to do it for all sorts of odds and sods, which didn't seem polite, and he wondered if Herman could have misheard.

A trim, smartly uniformed young woman stood at the foot of the steps. 'Mr Justice Slingsby?'

'That's me. Yes?'

'Will you follow me, please.'

He did, wondering what this was all about. Was

she taking him to be disembowelled by the vultures? She led him round to the side of the terminal building, where a taxi waited. A young woman in the back opened the door, smiled and beckoned him in. It was Janet!

She kissed him on the cheek – more than a peck – as he settled down by her.

'I'm very grateful,' said Ray, 'but what are you doing here? And where are we going?'

'To London. I thought it would be the easiest way to stop the press harassing you. I showed the airport authorities this and said I was in Special Branch, so they let you bypass Customs.' She waved her press card in front of him.

'Why are you doing this for me, Janet?'

Janet put on her most sincere expression, the one that on television meant she was about to ask a really awkward question. 'Because I like you Ray. And I think you've had a raw deal, and there could be worse to come.' Anyway, it was true. She did like the man, in spite of what she intended to do to him. During the previous evening she had almost begun to envy Sarah.

'What raw deal?'

'Being arrested. I mean, in your position.'

'Why weren't you arrested?'

'Chance. I was lucky.'

'You're going to a lot of trouble on my behalf.'

'I'm a friend. What's wrong with that?' She gave Ray a warmer kiss on the cheek, hoping to stop him asking awkward questions.

He felt he'd been here before, not long ago, and look what had happened then. But it was pleasant, this sudden attraction he seemed to hold for young women. Despite all that had happened, and was still going to happen, he didn't feel like stopping the car and getting out, though that's what his considered analysis of the situation told him he ought to do. Was he being weak again, or was he being sensible? Janet seemed to know her way around, and perhaps she could help him out. She was on the inside of the media, and they were enemy Number Two at the moment. Number One was Trot, gloating and rubbing his hands and looking forward to the execution, Ray was sure. Trotter had him by the balls and he'd squeeze till Ray yelled for mercy, which he had never done and never would.

He had never asked for any sort of consideration from 'them', except what he was entitled to. Against all the odds he had won his way to silk and the bench. He had survived against all Trotter and his men had thrown at him. This time things did seem stacked against him, but that's when you had to batten down the hatches or whatever, and he could do that, he'd done it since schooldays and always come through in the end.

Admittedly, this time it was different: it was definitely his own fault. He shouldn't have been such a fool in going to Ireland – it was a classic 'own goal'. But he'd fight and plan and manoeuvre to the last, and if he did go down he wouldn't surrender in the process. Trotter had to be resisted and might still be beaten. He was a man of clay – a Benito Mussolini who would strut and gesture and threaten till things got really hot and then he'd melt. Or would he? And how to turn the tables?

Ray made a sudden decision. 'Janet, stop the car.'

'Why?' Janet was alarmed.

'Tell him to take me back to Barfield.'

'But we're well on the way to London,' she protested.

'Then take me to the nearest railway station.'

'If you go back to Barfield, the press will crucify you, Ray. You need to lie low until the fuss dies down, and you need peace and quiet to work out how you're going to answer Trotter. Trust me, I know how these things work.'

'But I still don't know where you're taking me.'

Janet could tell that Ray was at least partially convinced, and she breathed a sigh of relief. The taxi was still heading for London. 'I've got a friend who's a foreign correspondent, and she's in South Africa for the next few weeks. When I'm in town I stay at her flat in East Finchley. She left me the key before she went. The press will never find you there. Nobody will.'

'But it's Monday the day after tomorrow. I should be sitting at Barfield Crown Court. And I'll have to tell Helen where I am.'

'Who rearranges things if you're ill?' asked Janet.

'Jack Woodford – my courts administrator.'

'Is he okay?'

'The administrators are mostly on my side, and he is. They loathe the people in London, like Trotter, who screw them down on salaries and bugger them about generally – treat them like cattle.'

'Have you Woodford's home number?'

Ray pulled out his address book and looked at it. 'Yes.'

'Then phone him when we get to London. Ask him to arrange a substitute – surely you can do that.'

He could, thought Ray. There were plenty of assistant recorders with their tongues hanging out for the daily sitting-fee as a deputy judge. It was easy money for unemployed barristers.

'And call your wife too,' Janet went on, 'but don't say what's happened. The less she knows the better at this stage. Tell her you're going to London with Billy on urgent legal business. She'll swallow that, won't she?'

She probably would, thought Ray gloomily. Helen trusted him. But for how much longer?

The taxi continued on its way. Soon it was leaving the M1 for the North Circular Road and Margaret Thatcher's old stamping-ground, Finchley. Ray reflected that in the days ahead he was going to need all the ex-PM's toughness and more subtlety than the Iron Lady had ever had – or she would not have suffered the chop, with which he, too, was now faced.

It was 12 noon and the Rt. Hon. Lord High Chancellor Trotter was feeling so good that there was only one appropriate place to express his feelings – in bed with his private secretary, Mrs Anona No-Knickers Chandelle-Sweet. Trot was in an excellent mood, and Anona felt happier herself. Her poor dope of a husband's prestigious appointment was about to be vindicated – if he was ever in a fit state to take it up again, which seemed doubtful according to the shrink at St Felix's. If not, at any rate she should come out of this affair in a stronger position than ever before, and able to negotiate an even grander pay-off should the worst come to the worst.

Even so, this didn't make her feel any more kindly toward the vast heaving bastard who at that very moment was forcing his prick in and out of her at a steady rate, giving her more pain than pleasure. It was a relief when he paused for a brief rest, even though she knew it would only prolong the agony.

'Slingsby's fucked at last,' Trot panted. He had been saying it at intervals all morning, but the pleasure it gave him to dwell on the subject never diminished. 'The next few days are going to be the most enjoyable I've ever had.'

'And what are you going to do?' asked Nonie. She had heard it all before, but she was humouring him in the hope that it would take his mind off sex.

'I shall announce it in the House on Monday. There'll be a motion that'll finally do for the bastard. I'll teach him to tell the world my appointments system is corrupt, and that *I* am too. It'll be a warning to any other judges who get big ideas. I'll rub the bastard's face in his own crap.'

'Then you won't have any enemies left, will you?'

'You don't think so, Nonie?' Trot frowned. 'There's still Harry Minnor. The PM doesn't like me. But he'll pipe down when he sees how I dispose of the Dishonourable Mr Justice bloody Raymond fucking Slingsby.'

Nonie had had enough. She wanted him off her as soon as possible. 'Are you going to finish fucking me, or aren't you? Because if not . . .'

Trot did finish. He strolled steadily towards the winning-post. He had never felt fitter. He was fighting fit. Fit to deal with all the fucking judges in the United Kingdom – yes even that stuck-up lot in Scotland, up there in their ivory tower – if they didn't toe the line. Between leisurely strokes, he said as much to Nonie.

'Aren't there any beyond the seas you can have a go at?' snapped Nonie, frustration and irritation getting the better of her.

Trot did not like her tone. 'Careful, Nonie. You're not the only private secretary in the land.'

'You just try getting rid of me,' she snarled, discretion forgotten. 'You might do it with Slingsby. But just try it with me and you'll be sorry.'

She had never felt such hatred for any man as at that moment. He still had his prick rammed into her and he could threaten her like that. There he was, grinding on and on, selfishly intent on his own pleasure and caring not a jot what she felt. At last he came, with more of a whimper than a bang. He rolled off immediately, removed the Durex and threw it on the carpet for his private secretary to pick up, dried his prick on a sheet and reached for

235

his underpants. He didn't need to search for his socks – he hadn't troubled to take them off.

Nonie, struggling into her own undergarments, watched him bend down with difficulty to pick up his shirt and thought what an obscene fat pig he was. If he tried putting that horrible dangling thing of his up her again she'd want telephone numbers in compensation, and she'd get them, one way or another. Trot seemed to think he had the drop on Slingsby, but she still had the drop on Trot. The way she felt at that moment, she'd be delirious if Slingsby could strike back at that great fleshy mountain of lard and cut it down to size. She had only met the judge once, but she quite liked him. He'd be a lot better in bed than Trot, she felt sure, and the thought gave her a faint frisson.

The phone rang. It was Kingston, informing his Lordship that Sir Malcolm Windsor had arrived for his appointment.

The Lord Chancellor apologised to the little proprietor of the *Courier* for keeping him waiting. He explained that he had had some important affairs of state to attend to, some difficult people to deal with, one in particular. There were some things one simply could not take lying down.

'Much better to stand up, my Lord. Much more comfortable,' agreed Sir Malcolm. 'Though of course sometimes one is forced to adopt a recumbent posture.'

Trot was puzzled. What was the newspaper magnate getting at? 'What is the purpose of your visit, Sir Malcolm?'

'I have had some news about you, Lord Trotter.'

Bloody hell, thought the Lord Chancellor. They haven't rumbled me, have they?

'It concerns Mr Justice Slingsby, a controversial figure, as you know.'

'Mr Justice Slingsby is well known to me,' said Trot stiffly, giving nothing away.

'I am not only the proprietor of the *Courier*, but also the editor-in-chief, a hands-on editor-in-chief. Some reliable information concerning the two of you has come into our possession. We intend to publish it on Monday.'

A devastating thought struck Trot like a torpedo. They'd done a David Mellor on him and put bugs in his bedroom or used long-distance lenses or something like that. He felt sick. Surely everything wasn't going to come unstuck, just when the victory parade was about to start?

He decided attack was the best form of defence. 'What lies has the *Courier* been told?'

'We understand that the judge has been to Ireland.'

'If he has,' said Trot pompously, 'he will be disciplined. A judge in his position should not undertake such a trip without asking my permission first.'

Sir Malcolm ignored this attempt to distract him. 'Someone who went with him – a most reliable woman journalist – indicates that there was a plot to trap the judge, discredit him. In short, to get him sacked.' Janet had said nothing of the kind, but Sir Malcolm had not got where he was today without being able to put two and two together. He knew all about the feud between the Lord Chancellor and Slingsby and he knew how much Lord Trotter would like to get rid of the socialist judge. He thought that Janet's whole story sounded extremely fishy and he guessed that it was a set-up. It was unlikely that the Lord Chancellor had actually organised the discrediting of Slingsby himself, but Sir Malcolm suspected that the plan might well have been inspired by someone close to him.'

'How appalling, Sir Malcolm. Who would want to do such a thing?' Trot was determined to give nothing away if he could help it.

Sir Malcolm's shrewd dark eyes studied him closely. He could see that he was sweating slightly. 'Our informant says it was you, Lord Chancellor.'

Trot's face went purple with suppressed rage. '*Me*. But why? What absolute nonsense.'

'That's why I have come here, in my capacity as editor-in-chief. In all fairness, we must have your version of the story, Lord Chancellor. We shall give it equal prominence, of course.'

'You seriously want me, the holder of the Great Seal, to take part in some sort of ridiculous fabrication for your scandal-sheet,' Trot exploded. 'Sir Malcolm, have you come here to insult me and waste my time? I've heard of the *Courier*, of course, but you'll forgive me if I don't regard it as essential reading for a busy Minister – and neither does anyone else whose opinion matters in this country. So publish and be damned, as Nelson said.'

'Wellington,' corrected Sir Malcolm. 'It was the

Duke of Wellington who said it.'

The confounded bloody nerve of the man, thought Trot. This uneducated upstart had insinuated his way into the country and somehow swindled his way into grabbing the appalling *Courier*. But a slimy little nothing from nowhere was not going to lecture the Lord Chancellor on British history, however many newspapers he owned.

'I don't give a damn *who* said it. *I* say it, and you ought to listen, Sir Malcolm Windsor, which I don't suppose for a moment is your real name. In your own interest, you had better not publish a lying story by some jumped-up journalist on the make.'

Sir Malcolm rose to his feet. 'Very good, Lord Chancellor. I have tried to do my duty by informing you. I am only sorry that you feel you cannot cooperate. I had hoped to be able to give our readers a balanced report, but if not ...' He shrugged, and turned towards the door.

Trotter recognised the implied threat, and wished he had not been so hasty. Sir Malcolm Windsor would be a powerful and ruthless enemy – he shouldn't have made that stupid remark about his name.

'Wait a moment, Sir Malcolm,' he said in a placatory tone. 'There's no need to rush into anything. Perhaps if you sat down and told me the full story, I could shed some light on it for you.'

Sir Malcolm smiled inwardly. He had the Lord Chancellor at a disadvantage now, which meant he was well on the way to getting what he wanted.

'We believe that your Lordship planned to put the judge in an incriminating position with a Page Three girl.'

'Let me see the proof, then.' Trot had not quite given up. 'Have you got photographs?'

The absence of photographs was a disadvantage to Sir Malcolm, but he wasn't going to admit to the Lord Chancellor that they didn't exist. 'I'm afraid I am not at liberty to release them at present.'

Trot sensed that he was stalling. 'I don't believe you've got any, which makes this whole tale worthless tittle-tattle. And who is this so-called journalist who is threatening to defame me in your newspaper? But no, don't tell me, or I might be tempted to report her – or him,' he added quickly, remembering that he was not supposed to know about any of this, 'to the police.'

'For what crime, my Lord?'

'Criminal libel. A very grave offence, especially when directed at one of Her Majesty's ministers. And libel is a civil matter also. The damages can be enormous.'

'We're well aware of that,' said Sir Malcolm. The *Courier* had had to pay out far too much in libel damages recently for his liking.

'You would be,' sneered Trot. 'The tabloids are stalwart supporters of the legal profession, aren't they?'

His tone stiffened Sir Malcolm's resolve. 'We have our lawyers, and you will have yours, Lord Chancellor. If you need them: you are a great lawyer yourself. The advice we have is to publish. Truth is a defence, as you know. You will read all about it in Monday's paper – if you send out for one.'

There was no need to be so arrogant, Trot thought. These immigrants behaved at though they ran the country, and the truth was, they very nearly did. And Sir Malcolm had a further shot that hit home. 'I have not become the proprietor of a great national newspaper by being afraid to do what I think is right, Lord Chancellor.'

He stood up and again made for the door. Trot called him back. 'There's no need to rush off, Sir Malcolm. We have a high regard here for the national press, and I allowed a full half-hour for this appointment. Do sit down, and we'll get you a coffee, or tea – or perhaps something stronger, eh?'

'You may not be very busy, sir, but I am.'

The bloody cheek of the man. He was rubbing it in now. They did that, these immigrants. He'd be taking the place over if he stayed much longer, but he couldn't be allowed to leave, as things stood. Trot renewed his offer of a drink.

'I will have a whisky on the rocks.'

Trot rang and ordered two, taking advantage of the opportunity to collect his thoughts. 'Please don't think this gossipy stuff worries me, Sir Malcolm,' he said, trying hard to sound calm. 'We get it all the time. Water off one's wig and all that. But I'm grateful to you for letting me know. I may say I've admired you for a long time. We need more of you people in this country.'

'I have been here some time. I am a British subject.' Sir Malcolm sounded offended.

'Of course you are,' said Trot hurriedly. 'Don't misunderstand me. I didn't put it very well, been working too hard. But you have done the state some service, as Macbeth said.'

'Othello, I think. I have studied our National Bard.'

'Evidently. What I'm driving at is, people like you, you do so much for our national life – employment for thousands and all that. *But it's not always appreciated.*'

Sir Malcolm Windsor sat up and took notice. This was more like it. 'And you think it should be?' he asked, looking closely at the Lord Chancellor.

'Her Majesty herself is always most anxious to recognise those who do outstanding service to the nation.'

'Ah, recognition.' Sir Malcolm brightened. 'And what form might this recognition take?'

'There are various options, obviously.'

'Had you the Order of Merit in mind, Lord Chancellor?'

Trot looked regretful. 'The number is limited, and there are no vacancies.'

'Companion of Honour?' Sir Malcolm asked hopefully.

Trot frowned. 'Possibly, but I would say you're too young, Sir Malcolm. It may come in due time. But a title – though I realise you have one already.'

'It was a great honour, to be knighted by Her Majesty herself,' said Sir Malcolm with enthusiasm. 'A wonderful lady. Buckingham Palace. A great day.'

'A gross injustice, if you hadn't had it.' Trot was laying it on thick now, sensing that he had hit on a way out of his problems with the newspaper proprietor. 'But you know, a knighthood is not the highest award that Her Majesty can bestow.'

'You're not by any chance thinking, Lord Chancellor, of a – peerage?' Sir Malcolm looked excited and he was.

'Such things are not distributed as freely as the free gifts offered by the *Courier*.'

'You are criticising us, Lord Chancellor?' A slight frown appeared on Sir Malcolm's swarthy face.

'No, no, no, please don't think that for a moment. I admire your newspaper. The courage when you take up issues of national importance. This country of ours needs that. Your organ does great service, and one is glad to mark that, er, appropriately.'

There was a pause as the whiskies arrived.

'Please understand this, Sir Malcolm,' Trot went on. 'Let there be no misunderstanding. Peerages are not two a penny. Her Majesty only confers them on those who merit them for outstanding service. You may well qualify – that would not surprise me at all. But I am not in a position to offer you anything, here and now. There is a committee that sifts these things most carefully. The Prime Minister himself, my good friend and colleague Harry Minnor, is always consulted and indeed his decision is naturally of paramount importance. Above all, a candidate – and there are many, many of them, believe me – is looked at

243

from every angle, his whole contribution to society is examined – good, and of course *bad*.'

'You are hinting something, Lord Chancellor,' Sir Malcolm suggested.

'No, no, believe me, that would be quite wrong. My word is only one among many, in a case like yours. But I must say, since you ask me, that, to take a hypothetical instance ... Well, for example, if you were considered by a consensus of the decision-makers to have taken some step that did not accord with the public interest, then naturally, the award could not go ahead.'

The *Courier*'s proprietor understood completely. 'You mean if I run this story, Lord Chancellor, then no peerage.'

Trot looked shocked. 'How could I possibly say that, Sir Malcolm? But if you are asking my advice, as I take it you are, I would indicate that a very promising situation could – *could* – be destroyed irrevocably.'

Sir Malcolm smiled. 'You can take it from me, as the editor-in-chief, that the story will not appear in the *Courier*, my Lord.'

And it didn't.

10

Ray and Janet spent Saturday and Sunday nights in separate bedrooms at the East Finchley flat, which was on the ground floor of a house in a long, ugly Victorian terrace. Both were very tired and took things easy, watching television, reading the papers and going for discreet strolls to the shops from time to time.

The first news relating to the Irish fiasco had already reached the newspapers. It was in the *Sunday Times* – copied by the rest of the Sunday press in their later editions. There was no reference to the trip itself, but the legal correspondent wrote that on the following day, in the House of Lords, the Lord Chancellor was to initiate a discussion on Mr Justice Slingsby's position, and there was speculation about a move to dismiss the judge. Revelations of a sensational kind were expected, but the Lord Chancellor's press office refused to comment.

Helen rang on Sunday afternoon, and it was Janet who answered the phone. Helen was worried about the press reports, and by the fact that reporters had been gathering at the Lodgings all day. They sought comments on the sacking rumours, and wanted to know where the judge was and if he had gone into hiding? Helen had refused to speak to them, she told Ray when he came to the phone, but she wanted to know what was going on. Precisely what had happened in Ireland, why had he rushed back in such a hurry, and what was he doing in London? Clearly there was more to this that he had told her when he phoned the previous evening.

Ray believed in speaking the truth, but for once he did his best to hold back. He said that while he and Billy were on their golfing trip, they happened to meet two Englishwomen whom Billy knew slightly. Billy then asked them back to the cottage for a meal. The Irish police had thought, farcically, that they were all terrorists, and had carried out a raid, but it had all been sorted out.

Not convinced, Helen probed further. Were the women intending to stay the night at the cottage? 'Not really,' said Ray weakly, which of course confirmed Helen's suspicions. She asked if the woman who had just answered the phone at the flat was one of the two in Ireland. 'Yes,' said Ray – the habit of honesty was just too strong.

This was too much for Helen. She had had her doubts about the expedition from the start, she told Ray. Anything involving Billy Wickstead-Hacking was bound to be suspect. She simply didn't believe the story about an accidental meeting with two women. They must have planned it between them from the start.

Her voice rose as the telephone tirade continued. Had Ray finally gone off his head, she asked? There was no other explanation for throwing overboard everything that should have mattered to him – his important job, his good name, her own trust. Through all their years of marriage she had tried to be a dutiful wife. She had looked after him, she had put up with his tantrums and eccentricities, and the embarrassment when he got into conflict – quite unnecessarily – with people like the Lord Chancellor.

She had been patient – Helen, normally so calm, was shouting now – but this was the final straw. She was not prepared to accept Ray going off on some mad sex expedition and coming back to disgrace her. And not even going home to her, but to another woman – sex-mad too, no doubt. The shame when everything hit the headlines, as it was bound to, would be too much. She had done all she could to keep their marriage on an even keel, but there were limits to what she could or should endure. What would her poor dead father the bishop have said? He was no longer there to share the shame, but her mother was and it was enough to kill an old lady of eighty-one. She intended to consult her solicitor at once, said Helen. Then she slammed down the phone before Ray had a chance to reply.

When he replaced the receiver, Ray felt as if he had been battered to the canvas; he was on his knees and nearly out for the count. Janet, seeing that he had gone pale, patted his shoulder and tried to comfort him. Everything would be all right, she told him, if he kept his nerve. She would take him to a nice little Sardinian restaurant round the corner for dinner and Ray would feel better after a good meal and some red wine. Everybody had their troubles, and it wasn't always easy to stand back and see them in perspective.

Ray said wryly that it certainly wasn't easy to see in perspective the simultaneous loss of his job, his marriage and his reputation, not forgetting his pension. What could be worse?

'You could be dead,' Janet suggested.

Ray groaned. 'Would that be worse? I wouldn't suffer any longer.'

'You could lose your daughter. While you have life you can fight the people who are trying to do you down.'

'They don't need to try very hard when I seem to be helping them like this.' Ray sat on the sofa with his head in his hands, the picture of despair.

'You can start again, if it comes to it. I had to. My husband walked out and landed me with all our debts. I lost my permanent job and had to go freelance. I'm still fighting back – I haven't succeeded yet.'

Janet wasn't sure if Ray was listening, but she kept talking. Telling him about the mess she had made of her own life might make him feel better, she thought. She explained about her financial problems and her fragmented life with no stability at the centre. She had been looking for someone she could trust and share things with. Instead she had fallen in with people like Billy Wickstead-

Hacking and let them use her. She'd like to get married again, and have children, but that seemed an impossible dream. At times she had been near to despair.

So Ray wasn't alone with his problems, she went on. And the struggle with Trotter wasn't over. Helen would come round, Janet was sure. She didn't sound the type to do anything final, whatever she said on the phone. Helen wouldn't condemn herself to a solitary old age by deserting her husband, and she was unlikely to find another man now. Or want one, Ray added bitterly.

'If Helen does leave you, will you really mind?' asked Janet.

Ray tried to be truthful. 'Despite everything – the lack of real rapport, our different attitudes to life – about sex especially – Helen did me no wrong, not deliberately. We lived together in a kind of complacent amity.'

'But if you lost your marriage, it wouldn't be the end of the world – or you wouldn't have gone to Ireland.'

Ray pondered this idea as Janet, the TV interviewer, widened the focus of her questioning. 'Suppose you do lose your job, will you miss it?'

'In one way, I don't think I would,' he said slowly. 'I didn't set out in life wanting to be a judge. I wanted to be a barrister because I'm an argumentative sort of person; I like discussing things. I never dreamt in those distant days that I'd end up on the bench. But a barrister in his late forties has to decide whether to soldier on, winding down as his younger colleagues overtake him, or opt for the security that the bench provides. When you're young you're eager and hungry and you don't mind sitting up all night absorbing a brief that was delivered late, thinking up fresh phrases, new ways to demolish the other side. But eventually there's nothing new any more. The eagerness goes. You've heard it all and seen it all. And a lot of work I had at the Bar was for worthless people – obviously guilty defendants – dangerous, some of them, and I had to strive to free them and let them harm more innocent victims.'

'But now you're fed up with the bench too,' Janet pointed out. 'Is it something inside you? Are you restless?'

Ray grimaced. There was far more to it than that. 'Britain has become a land fit for criminals to live in. We are ruled by spineless politicians and gutless judges. Politicians seize on any device to reduce the prison population: parole, suspended sentences. They're obsessed with statistics and they don't care whether wicked people get the clobbering they deserve, or the innocent are protected and avenged. The judges fall into line like a herd of conformist sheep, and do you know why?'

'Trotter?' guessed Janet.

'Precisely. That's why I'm cynical about my job. It's the system lord chancellors have for appointing and promoting and controlling judges. They go for safe, conformist people, who can be relied on to toe the official line. What happens to a judge who speaks out and wants to buck the system?'

Janet knew the answer to that only too well. 'It's what's happening to you, Ray.'

'I've done my best to make a stand,' Ray said, 'but I haven't enjoyed the life all that much. I haven't felt comfortable.'

'If the worst does happen, what will you do?'

Ray shrugged. 'I can't go back to the Bar – it isn't allowed. Any pension will be discretionary – and we know about Trotter's discretion. I have some savings, but I'm not rich.'

'You may have to give up the fine house and the grand life.'

'I shall be back where I started, with nothing: Raymond Slingsby, son of a coal-miner, making my own way, dreaming my own dreams.'

'Tell me about your dreams, Ray,' said Janet softly. She was fascinated by what she was hearing. This was probably the best interview she had ever done.

Ray stared into space, as if seeing a vision of an alternative future. 'Maybe I should have been an artist. I still paint, but I haven't pursued it as I should have done. Not like Paul Gauguin.'

'With his dusky maidens. Is that part of your dreams?'

'The truly happy man is the creative artist. He is wrapped up in the process of creation, away from the world and its petty problems. He is making something unique that will be there after he has gone. It can be a painting, a sculpture, a book, or a building, a piece of furniture. But he – or she – they put all they have into it, and while they are enthralled in the process there is no time to sit and think about the futility of life.' Ray paused for a moment, looking sad. 'That's what life is in the end,' he went on. 'A nothing, a decline into death and oblivion. But you don't think about that when you are creating. Compare that with sitting in a musty courtroom listening to petty people's problems and trying to solve them, within the law's narrow limits.'

'But you chose the life,' Janet couldn't help pointing out.

'I drifted into it. I've sometimes thought of giving it up, burning that absurd eighteenth-century wig and scarlet-and-ermine robe, and selling everything. I'd like to buy a yacht, sail to the Mediterranean, to be on deck in the sun with the smooth swirl of the sea under the hull, and the wine, and the colours of the islands, and – painting.'

'But you were chained to Helen.'

'To a corpse, Janet. Not a corpse of a person but a corpse of a marriage. And it's still my destiny.'

'You daren't leave the old life, unless they force you to,' challenged Janet.

'I couldn't make a living by painting.'

'Life on a boat is simple. You could wash dishes, if necessary. But you have been corrupted by the high life, haven't you, Ray?'

She was trying to provoke him, but Ray was not to be drawn. 'No, Janet,' he said seriously, 'it's not so simple. I can't quit now, that's all. If I lose, I'll face it, but I've never been a quitter.'

There was a long pause. Then Janet sighed, stood up and suggested they go out for dinner.

They went to the Sardinian place, which had checked tablecloths and candles on the tables, and drank two bottles of red wine with their pasta before returning to their separate bedrooms. Ray slept well, which surprised him.

At two o'clock on Monday Janet and Ray were sitting on the sofa after their Chinese take-away lunch. The TV set was on BBC 2 and an unseen woman was presenting the House of Lords to the nation. The television cameras showed some of the lords and ladies waiting for the debate to begin. Though the presenter did not say so, they were of various kinds. Many had been appointed by a prime minister – rewarded for past service as ministers, put out to grass after disservice, or sent there to provide a safe by-election for an important politician who had lost his or her own seat.

Others were there because some forebear had been granted the right for himself, his heirs and successors to legislate by a king grateful for his wife's favours in bed. Yet others took their place because father or grandfather had benefited by the Liberal Prime Minister David Lloyd George's propensity to bestow peerages on wealthy industrialists in return for large but discreet contributions to Liberal party funds. Then there were a few law lords because, by a strange historical anomaly, the House of Lords happened to be the final appellate court, and a clever select few of Her Majesty's judges ended their careers there.

Most of their lordships and ladyships were already seen by the viewers to be settling into various stages of slumber. This was especially true of those who were only there to kill time and collect the welcome daily attendance allowance. Those still partially awake chatted quietly as they waited for the big moment.

Several government ministers from the Commons, including the PM himself, sat on the steps to the Throne. These were technically outside the chamber as was – by an unbelievable medieval quirk – the Woolsack itself, on which the Lord Chancellor presided over the House. Another oddity was that the Lord Chancellor had no disciplinary powers and peers while on their feet did not address him but each other.

The Lord Chancellor could not call on a peer to resume his seat; the only way to shut up a speaker who went on too long, as most did on most occasions, was for someone to move 'that the noble lord – or lady – be no longer heard', and that was then voted on. Foreigners used to wonder how a nation so legislated for had managed to stagger into the twenty-first century, and the answer was that it hadn't. Little had changed for centuries, which was what the country was about – preserving itself as a floating antique-shop. That was Raymond's thought, as he watched Lord Trotter rise. There was a hush, broken only by subdued rhythmical snoring.

The Lord Chancellor read from a script that Sir Anthony Kingston had prepared, assisted by Mrs Anona Chandelle-Sweet.

'Your Lordships will understand my anxiety,' he began, 'as I rise to my feet this day, that this whole House should rise to the full dignity and solemnity necessitated by its ancient rights and privileges.'

At this point, Lord Blanchit-Withers of the Pennines, shouted 'Hear hear' four times. Previously known in trade union circles as Tom White, for a short time the Tory MP for Pennines Central, Lord Blanchit-Withers had recently been ennobled to provide a safe seat, that unfortunately turned out to be unsafe, for a former minister named Harry Rankith, who had lost his own seat at the general election.

Lord Blanchit-Withers was determined to make his mark early, but he was timid about launching into his maiden speech – his only words recorded in Hansard during his few months as an MP had been 'Mr Speaker, it is very stuffy in here. There is far too much hot air. Could we have the windows open?' No-one knew whether he had been trying to be humorous, although some people gave him the benefit of the doubt. But he had come to emphasise his presence by saying 'Hear hear' four times instead of the usual twice, and had brought this habit with him to the Lords.

The Lord Chancellor continued, 'As I was saying, my Lords, or was about to say, the judiciary in this ancient land of ours has always held a high place in the affections of the people and the respect of this House and of another place. And I am gratified to know, as I would expect from my long service in your Lordships' House, that your Lordships are at one accord with one another and indeed with myself, as indeed I am with your Lordships. And as I would expect from your Lordships' ancient House . . . '

There was a pause here. The Lord Chancellor had lost his place in the script, Kingston having scribbled several last-minute amendments and improvements. Trot was saved however, as the House knew from previous experience that it was their fraternal duty to cover up for him, which they all, with a few exceptions, did by repeatedly calling out 'Hear hear'.

The Lord Chancellor found his place and pressed on. 'I am gratified to have your Lordships' unanimous support at this momentous moment. As I was saying, or was about to say, judicial independence may fairly be said to have been established by the Bill of Rights of 1689. In 1700, however, Parliament made the judges secure beyond doubt or peradventure from interference by the Executive, by passing the Act of Settlement which finally set the seal on the 1688 Glorious Revolution.'

At this point there were more 'Hear hears', four times from Lord Blanchit-Withers, who, though half asleep, responded as always to the word 'Revolution' like one of Pavlov's salivating dogs. In his youth he had been a left-wing trade-unionist, and he only became a right-wing Tory trade-unionist MP to forestall his inevitable sacking from the post of general secretary to the Union of Sword-swallowers, Knife-throwers and Plate-spinners, which had broken away from the

Actors' Union and, after eighteen months under White, was broken in members, in the spirit of those few who survived, and at the bank.

Tom always retained a hankering after his left-wing connections, although he himself believed in nothing except self-promotion, like most politicians. He was welcomed by the Tories as proof that they were not all snobs, though Tom soon found that they *were* and rather than try to change them he became one himself.

'My Lords, the 1700 Act established for all time that a High Court judge is and will always be independent, by requiring an address by both Houses to the Sovereign for his dismissal,' the Lord Chancellor continued his historical lesson. 'That protection was not afforded to Circuit judges by the Courts Act 1971, which was drafted by my noble and learned predecessor, Lord Hailsham.'

Ray and Janet looked at one another, and Janet put a reassuring hand in Ray's as they listened.

'My right honourable and learned friend Lord Hailsham, when drafting the 1971 Act, permitted the Lord Chancellor to remove a Circuit judge for misbehaviour. It might have been wiser for our noble predecessors in 1700 to do the same with High Court judges.'

'Hear, hear,' from those still awake.

'But we must accept and act on that legislation until it is changed, and what I am about to say may make us think that should be soon.'

Lord Blanchit-Withers woke up with a start, thinking he was at a Tory party conference, which was almost the case. 'That's a load of crap!' he said automatically.

'I did not hear the unfortunate remark that fell from my honourable and noble friend Lord Blanchit-Withers,' said the Lord Chancellor in a frosty voice.

'A load of crap, I said, Mr Chairman,' shouted the former trade-unionist.

There were cries of 'Oh!' 'Shame!' 'Order!' from around the chamber. 'The man should be horsewhipped,' shouted Lord Kensington.

'And you too, you pompous socialist fathead,' retorted Lord Blanchit-Withers, getting excited by the debate.

The Lord Chancellor started to look flustered. 'I must earnestly appeal to this House for calm on this solemn occasion,' he urged. Fumbling with his papers again, he went on, 'But to return to the Honourable Mr Justice Raymond Slingsby.'

'How can you return to him? You haven't mentioned him yet. Get on with it, for God's sake, man,' cried Lord Smith of Smithfield.

At this point eleven peers woke up, stood up, looked around, gazed at the clock, compared it with their own watches and walked out of the Chamber in a shambling line, like the England cricket eleven leaving the field after a typical day against the Pakistan eleven. Others of their lordships and ladyships had already left the Chamber and now there were only about two dozen remaining, most of whom were asleep.

Janet turned to Ray, smiled put her thumbs up and kissed him on both cheeks. The kisses were more than pecks and less than passionate declarations.

The Lord Chancellor ploughed on to his diminished audience, 'I have known Raymond Slingsby for many years. Let me be fair as well as frank. He has some high qualities, including eloquence and a good brain. But, my Lords, such qualities are not of necessity sufficient for the due discharge of the ancient and honourable office of High Court judge.'

'Do get on with it!' pleaded Lord Bloreham of Bessingborough. 'Tell us what this judge has been up to.'

'I am deeply obliged to my honourable noble and learned friend,' said a tight-lipped Lord Chancellor. 'Mr Justice Slingsby, I regret to inform this House, has unfortunately failed to live up to our ancient traditions.'

'He isn't a member of this House, is he?' Lord Bloreham looked confused. 'Or are you going to make him one? And I speak as the most senior member of this House.'

'What about Binkie Thackersfield?' shouted someone.

The white-haired Lord Bloreham looked offended. 'To my recollection, the noble Lord just referred to has not set foot in this House since the end of the Second World War. I have myself been here every day since, er . . .'

'Since daily allowances came in,' came a voice.

'I really must insist, my Lords,' pleaded the Lord Chancellor, trying to get on with his speech. 'Unhappily for the nation, for the judiciary as a whole and finally for myself, Mr Justice Slingsby has acted with extreme folly. I must not shrink from that word, or indeed from "irresponsibility" or any other word that from time to time may be deemed to be, er . . .'

His voice trailed away as he watched a further dozen or so peers and peeresses shuffle out. The House now consisted of seven members. Lady Baxter-Onslow-Stoppe (Conservative) who had been recumbent for some time, started to snore so loudly that Lady Blethers (Labour/Liberal Democrat) screwed up her order-paper and stuffed it down the noble throat of the snoring peeress. The snoring noises intensified as the Lord Chancellor droned on again, until all at once Lady Baxter-Onslow-Stoppe fell from her leather seat and lay writhing and groaning on the carpeted floor. The Lord Chancellor hesitated. This was an unprecedented situation in the history of the ancient House. Happily he received some good advice from the honourable and noble Lord Beacon of Breckon who had just entered the Chamber, having spent several hours in another part of the building.

'I shay shuspend the shitting.' Lord Beacon lurched into his seat and fell asleep at once.

'Excellent idea,' said the Lord Chancellor with relief. 'The sitting is suspended for a quarter of an hour.'

The lady announcer's voice returned, 'And so we have to leave this important debate in the House of Lords, which of course has been of the high standard we have learnt to expect from that

260

ancient House. Our next programme is a film on life in Britain during the Stone Age.'

'Will we notice any difference?' said Ray Slingsby.

Lord Chancellor Trotter was apprehensive when he heard that Lord Chief Justice Jonathan Black was coming to see him on Monday evening as a matter of urgency. As Chancellor he was head of the judicial system and appointed judges, but he was himself a politician appointed by and removable by the Prime Minister. He left office when another party came to power.

The Lord Chief Justice was appointed by the Lord Chancellor after consulting the Prime Minister. He headed the criminal justice system and spoke for the judges on important occasions. Trot had 'inherited' Black and on the few occasions they had met had found him formidable. He was not only a strong and capable advocate, but had a grammar school education. He was not one of the safe public-school C. of E. people whom the Establishment could always rely on as conformist. You didn't know where you were with men like Black, they spoke a different language.

The most disturbing feature of all was that a lord chief justice had a unique position: he had no higher to climb and so there were no levers to apply to him. Most judges were pliable, because they wanted something, if only promotion to the Court of Appeal and then the House of Lords. The Lord Chief Justice was in his job until he retired, unless he did something such as Slingsby had done, but there was no suspicion that he was addicted to any vices except work – a surprising thing but not sufficient to have him dismissed.

Lord Black got straight down to business in his direct northern way, without frills or pleasantries. 'Lord Chancellor, I think you should have told me before raising the matter of Mr Justice Slingsby in the House this afternoon. I could not be there – I was hearing an urgent case that was part-heard.'

'You knew we were having difficulties with Slingsby, Lord Chief.' Trot was always polite to Lord Black.

'There *are* difficulties with judges, because they are people. And we all know Ray Slingsby has certain views that some people disagree with, yourself included. He may be indiscreet at times. But to raise it in that way was wrong, in my view. You should have spoken to me first.'

'I do, as to appointments.'

'Not on the Chandelle-Sweet one,' said Lord Black grimly.

'It was a special case, Lord Chief,' pleaded Trot.

'That is the general view of the judges. An extraordinary case.'

Trot tried to justify himself. 'I must do my duty as I see it.'

'I am prepared to raise the Slingsby matter in the House if you wish, Lord Chancellor,' said Lord Black.

'No, no, no. There is no need for that.'

Lord Black looked at Trot severely. 'Do you realise that you have laid yourself open to an application by Slingsby for a judicial review – to set aside your decision to refer the matter to Parliament?'

'We were not aware of that.' It cost Trot a lot to admit this and even more to ask, 'What can we do about it?'

'At the very least you should give Slingsby notice of what is alleged against him, and an opportunity to reply. We call that natural justice.'

'I shall do exactly as you suggest, Lord Chief,' said Trot humbly.

'It must be done before the House of Commons considers the matter,' Lord Black warned. 'And you should have a shorthand-note taken.'

'I will. And the judge shall have a copy.'

Lord Black rose to his considerable height, nodded and departed. What a very dangerous man, Trot thought. Like a nuclear device against which there is no defence. Not a man I wish to cross swords with, but it's always the honest ones who are the most dangerous. I'll do as he says – not that it'll make any difference to the result.

On Monday evening Ray and Janet dined at the flat and the atmosphere between them was sombre. Later that afternoon, the House of Lords had managed to obtain a quorum and pass the motion to petition Her Majesty to dismiss Mr Justice Slingsby. The Commons were expected to complete the process, though a news item had announced that the Lord Chancellor was to give the judge an opportunity to put his case on the following day. Ray had decided to fight Trotter to the end, though he knew his chances were slim. He was against the ropes, with two tough rounds to go.

'Ray, there is one way you can defend yourself and counter-attack,' suggested Janet, watching Ray staring moodily into his coffee cup. 'The media. You can get them on your side.'

'How would I do that?' Ray looked unimpressed by the idea.

'Go to the tabloids. They have power. They finished David Mellor. They could topple Trotter, or help to.'

'Have you been in touch with any of them since Ireland, Janet?' he asked suspiciously.

'I spoke to Bob Bamford, editor of the *Courier*,' admitted Janet.

'To sell him the story?'

'I am a journalist,' she said, her expression defiant.

Ray stared at her. 'Is that your motive? Is that why you've gone to all this trouble to bring me here and say you want to help me? Because you want to sell the story? For a big sum, presumably. What have you agreed with the *Courier*? Come on, Janet, I must know. Whose side are you on?'

'Yours, Ray.' She desperately wanted him to believe her.

'How much have you been paid?' Ray continued grimly.

Janet hesitated. 'A thousand from the *Courier*. But then they cried off. There's the *Sun*, the *Mirror*, but I haven't tried them yet.'

'There'll be a lot more cash in it, if you can get

my story too. Is that what it's all been about, Janet?'

She turned her head away and would not answer.

'Janet? Look at me.'

Janet forced herself to look at Ray. 'There's something I have to tell you. It isn't easy, but I owe it to you. The Irish trip was a set-up. Trotter and Kingston got Billy to take you there with Sarah, so they could get pictures of you on the job with her.'

'To blackmail me into resigning.' Ray saw it all now. Janet's words confirmed the worries that had been gnawing away at him on and off ever since Billy had suggested the Irish trip.

'I suppose so.'

'And who was going to take the photographs? Not you, Janet?'

Janet hung her head. 'That's why I went upstairs – for my camera.'

Ray was white with anger. 'Janet, how could you? I've trusted you. I liked you. I thought you wanted to help me because *you* liked *me*.'

'But I do, Ray,' Janet insisted.

'Enough to stab me in the back,' snorted Ray. 'It didn't work in Ireland, so you brought me here, to make money out of me by getting me to go to the press with my story, putting up the price for yours.'

Janet was sobbing quietly.

'Is that what women are?' he continued remorselessly. 'I'm learning a lot about them all of a sudden. You are devious. You use people, just as much as some men do women – men like your boy-friend Billy Wickstead-Hacking. A fine pair you make, you two. A sleazy couple on the make. He wanted – what? – from Trotter. A judgeship?'

Janet nodded through her tears.

'What a fool I've been. With my eyes open I set out to betray my wife, a nice woman who'd done me no wrong. And I find I'm being used by three unscrupulous people.'

'Not Sarah,' protested Janet. 'She didn't know.'

'There must have been something in it for her. She can't have fancied a foolish old man. Why am I so naive? I've spent all these years delving into people's minds. I should have known that Billy never did a decent thing in his life. But you, Janet, I thought you were different. Instead, the helping hand you put on my shoulder had a knife in it.'

'It wasn't like that, Ray.' Janet's sobbing increased in force.

'You know Janet, you could be up at the Old Bailey for what you did in Ireland – the conspiracy. You'd get at least five years.'

'I was short of money,' Janet pleaded. 'You don't know how desperate I was.'

'Money!' exclaimed Ray furiously. 'Why has everything to be judged in terms of money these days? That's all most people ever seem to think about. Take politicians. What else do they think about except lining their pockets? Oh, they talk about ideals and service, but that's just talk. Look at them carefully. They're after money for directorships, articles in the press, freebies abroad, and – yes – sex. I know I'm guilty too, about the sex part; it's led me to my own destruction. But at least I haven't been dragged down by lust for money. I wanted a good time when I went to Ireland and, yes, sex was the main part of it, but I thought there was something romantic to it as well. Absurd, of course. I'd have woken up one morning and known how absurd it was. But it wasn't sordid, it wasn't entirely sordid. And there was no financial grubbiness about it at all.'

Janet was now crying bitterly. She admired this man and she was ashamed for herself as she had never been before. Through her sobs she tried to explain. 'I'm in debt, Ray. That's no excuse. But I owe the building society and the bank. I did hope for money out of it, a lot of money. And I'm ashamed. Deeply ashamed.'

She paused, gulping for breath, tears running down her cheeks. Ray was looking at her with a strange expression on his face, as if his tirade had used up all his fury against her. For a long moment they stared into each other's eyes. Then Janet leaned over and kissed him on the lips.

Ray responded instinctively. The part of his rational mind that remained in control told him that this was ridiculous. He had virtually ruined himself with Sarah, yet here he was committing the same sin – or about to, if he could. He told himself to stop, but he knew he did not want to.

They slid to the carpet and lay together as their tongues flicked and felt and tasted and advanced and withdrew. Instinctively he began to fondle her. She did not resist, but murmured a suggestion that they move to her bedroom. There Ray slowly removed Janet's clothing, garment by garment,

taking his time and determined to get it right this
time, from the delicious beginning to what he
hoped would be the delirious crescendo.

He felt much more confident than he had been
at this stage with Sarah. Janet was older, more
experienced – she knew the litany of sex, the ways
and wants of men. Janet herself was eager to give
this man what he wanted and needed. Good men,
decent men of principle, were rare and she
wondered if she had ever met one before, but here
was one now. She had wronged him shamefully
and shamelessly, done things to him he did not
deserve. Now she would do things to him and for
him that he wanted her to do and he, she hoped
and suspected, would return her tenderness with
loving. She was in Ray's debt, and she would
repay it with interest, in the way a woman can
repay a man, with her whole body, her whole
nakedness, her whole being. Mr Justice Slingsby
had never felt so gloriously in charge yet out of
control, even when trying the most dramatic High
Court libel or Crown Court murder. This was what
he had yearned for so long: a mature woman who
knew, who understood what he wanted and
needed. With Sarah it had gone off at half-cock or
would have done, but Janet was different, as he
felt his body acknowledge already. As a barrister
and then a judge Ray had had to be careful,
hesitant, balanced, restrained, in control at all
times. Now the sandcastle of his mind was being
flattened and swamped by seas of emotion, and
though he feared the consequences he luxuriated
in the feeling.

Even he, rebel as he was, had always been compelled to rein himself in, hold himself back, constipated, dressing in suits and gowns of formal black, wearing clean stiff white collars. He had been regimented. Lawyers had ancient rules and practices and there was no freshness, no spontaneity, no change. It was the same in his life away from the courts. Middle-class society had had him by the throat, compelling him to conform or be isolated, and in the end he had done both.

In the sexual field Ray had never really done more than kick around odd balls; he had never played a full-length match, until now with Janet Yorke. And not against her but with her, passing and feinting and centring and aiming for the net and finding it, together. That had never happened to him before – his emotions had been so carefully guarded, so dammed, stagnant, sterile.

Now Ray was released in one delicious undammed roaring flood, and he was happy. Was he in love with Janet, he asked himself, and was he not too carried away to know that it was much too soon to say. But he liked her, very much, and he would never be the same dead tree of a man that he had been before. Here were new green shoots. Whatever happened in the next day or two between himself and Trotter, even if he were ruined, humiliated, shamed and shunned by the world and by Helen, it did not matter so much now. When all seemed hopeless, he had learnt to live.

As he lay in peace in Janet's arms, he wondered what was to happen in the confrontation Ray

Slingsby *v* Lord Chancellor Trotter? Even now he was not going to hold up his hands, surrender and throw himself on Trot's mercy. The man didn't have any mercy, he'd demand every ounce of flesh, every shred of triumph. The odds were still against Ray, and he was alone, with no barrister or judge daring to ally themselves to him. No journalist either, until this moment, but he would fight on because he had never known any other way.

Ray kissed Janet, who murmured sleepily and happily, then stretched an arm out of bed to turn on the radio. It was time for the news, and he soon heard that, the Lords having voted for his dismissal, the Commons were to debate a similar motion by the Prime Minister in two days' time. The large Tory majority in the House made it virtually certain that the first English High Court judge would be dismissed, although the Lord Chancellor had issued a statement saying that he had decided to hear the judge's case personally and transmit the resultant transcript to the Commons for them to consider. He was most anxious to be scrupulously fair to Mr Justice Slingsby, Lord Trotter said.

11

LORD HIGH and Mighty Bloody Trotter, as his private secretary had started to call him when speaking to others, was slightly ashamed of himself and more than slightly disgusted with her. He had just accused her, at a vital moment, of a lack of enthusiasm, and she had actually bitten the tender end of his prick.

It had not drawn blood, but it hurt and he instinctively thought of suing her. However he soon abandoned the notion when he considered the obvious evidential hurdles, including having to exhibit the offended organ, even in the privacy of his chambers, to a judge he himself had probably appointed. The indignity in such a proceeding would outweigh his satisfaction at seeing Nonie pillaged by an order for damages.

As for a criminal charge – assault occasioning actual bodily harm, or at the least common assault – that would be in the Magistrates' Court, an even less acceptable tribunal. But Trot would get his revenge on his rebellious secretary in one way or another. He would like to set some sort of trap for her, in order to have the satisfaction of sacking her without any financial come-back on her part. Unfortunately the best person to think up such a plan was Nonie herself, and Trot could not ask her to plot her own downfall. So he lay silently and sullenly beside her, massaging his wounded prick with Vaseline.

It really *was* time to get another private secretary, he vowed, and he would select one young enough to make a strictly controlled diet one of the conditions of her contract. Anona Chandelle-Sweet was a glutton, and the results were becoming more and more obvious. As soon as the Slingsby thing was over – tomorrow, almost certainly – and things had gone quiet, he would somehow arrange to have her transferred to the most unpleasant Minister he could think of.

Terence Whitstable, the current Minister for Recreation, Drought and Rain, was a possible candidate. Terry had been a soccer blue at Cambridge and had made his name in a match against Oxford that was billed as 'friendly' and was, until Terry kicked their goalie in the goolies. The effects of his kick put the keeper in hospital, Oxford were forced to play their reserve striker in his place, and Terry was able to score five goals in quick succession.

The chairman of the Tory party thought such unscrupulous gamesmanship qualified Terry for a distinguished parliamentary career. He was soon found a safe seat, and he excelled himself in the Commons, committing professional fouls at question-time in the shape of points of order that were nothing of the kind, and shouting carefully thought-out abuse at opponents who raised genuine points. Such a man would go far, and at thirty-one he was already Minister for Recreation and universally loathed by his subordinates.

The transfer would have to be handled carefully, or Anona Chandelle-Sweet – how unpleasant that name tasted in his mind now – would go to those confounded tabloids, shooting her mouth off about him. Would they dare to print it? Yes, at least one of them would. The trouble was he couldn't possibly fix them all because two of their proprietors were already peers, and he was at a loss to know how to top that.

'Nonie?' He tried to sound pleasant.

'You can fuck off. You're not getting any more,' his secretary said rudely, turning her back on him.

'You're much too fat, you know.' His Lordship gave up his effort to be conciliatory almost before it had begun.

'And you're a great big slob, Trot. So shut up and leave me alone.' Nonie pulled the pillow over her head.

'How dare you say that to me?' It was a weak shot, and his next was even weaker. 'And you can stop calling me Trot.'

Nonie lifted the pillow a fraction. 'It's the politest thing anybody does call you.'

'You bitch.' Trot descended to insults again. 'You had a body once. Look at those boobs. Once they faced mankind with pride. Now they're almost round your waist, like some great big African woman. As for your arse, it's just a lump

273

of shivering lard. You disgust me, you really do.'

She flung the pillow aside. 'Who are you to talk, you fat trotting toad!'

'I happen to be your employer, Anona.'

Nonie sat up, furious. 'And you happen to have been fucking me for the last two and a half years,' she shouted.

'You needn't think fucking is the basis for intimacy.' Trot thought the remark a clever one and having, as he saw it, finally won the point, he decided to end the debate by getting out of bed. As he bent to pick up his socks, his private secretary, who had followed him, kicked him hard on the rump sending him sprawling.

Livid and purple-faced, he hauled himself to his feet. 'You wait! You just wait, No-Knickers. Good name for you, that. Lower your knickers for anybody for half-a-crown. That's the news I heard.'

'Must be old bloody news,' she jeered. 'Half-crowns went out years ago. And has anybody ever told you how fucking awful you are in bed? Even that feeble husband of mine is better at it than you are.'

Trot's body shook and shivered with indignation. 'Get dressed immediately, Mrs Chandelle-Sweet. Go downstairs. There's important work for you. Go and prepare yourself, and start by shutting that cesspit of a mouth.'

'Bollocks to you, Lord Chancellor!' retorted Nonie succinctly, retreating to the far side of the bed where she started to collect her scattered clothes.

Lord Trotter thought it beneath his dignity to banter further – and he had run out of suitable insults. So he dressed in what he intended to be a dignified silence, then went downstairs to his office to face the most crucial day of his life. He was about to meet Mr Justice Slingsby, face to face, and finally settle the account between them. Then he would be free to think of a suitable way of dealing with his unacceptably disloyal private secretary.

Lord Chancellor Trotter sat at his capacious desk and addressed his troops – Sir Anthony Kingston KCB and Mrs Anona Chandelle-now-not-so-Sweet. The desk had been carefully cleared for the approaching conflict. Kingston had all relevant documents stacked neatly to one side, including the bulging official file on that black sheep of the judiciary, the Honourable Mr Justice Raymond Slingsby, and a thinner file on the most lightweight, indeed almost weightless, member of the Circuit bench, his Honour Judge Alwyne Chandelle-Sweet.

The Lord Chancellor began with a lengthy justification for the imminent hearing in the case of the People versus Slingsby.

Kingston, as usual, had a correction for him. 'If I may say so with all due diffidence, Lord Chancellor, we never use the concept "the People", although they do in the United States, where democracy is taken to lengths we would not tolerate.'

'Oh, really?' said Trotter, staring at him.

Taking this as a request for further information, Kingston explained that it had been a dreadful mistake for Americans to expel King George III. The colonists were British and the King was the King, and that was how it should have remained.

'How very interesting,' the Lord Chancellor said, with heavy irony, as his permanent secretary went on to attack the US Senate's right to veto the President's choice of Supreme Court judges. That showed, he said, to what depths democracy had sunk in the country after the British were so rudely expelled. To let non-judges veto judges chosen by the elected head of the nation was reminiscent of the Russian Revolution.

'Shut up, Kingston,' exploded the Lord Chancellor, 'and don't speak until you're spoken to. Better still, don't speak at all – just make a note to have yourself transferred to the Ministry of Recreation, Drought and Rain. It's the only place for a cricket-playing wet like you.'

Obediently Kingston shut up and made the note in his careful handwriting, privately telling himself that any ministry would be preferable to this one, presided over as it was by a bad-tempered buffoon who became loonier by the day.

'This is the big one.' Trotter looked around to check that his subordinates were suitably impressed. 'We have to win this Slingsby thing, or all control over judges will end. They will think they are independent and can do justice according to their own consciences. Well, they can't, they can do it according to mine, or get booted out. The country is going to the dogs, and people like

Raymond Slingsby are barking up the wrong tree.'

Kingston had a question for him. 'What roles do you wish *us* two to play, sir?'

'This is a unique ball-game. We have to play it by ear. Mrs Chandelle-Sweet will take a short-hand-note of the entire proceedings.'

'You want me to take everything down?' The idea alarmed Nonie – she hadn't had much opportunity to practise her shorthand recently.

Trot thought of a tart riposte, but suppressed it. 'It must be written down. The transcript must make clear that Slingsby has been granted every opportunity to present his case.'

'Or he might apply to the High Court and get the whole thing quashed,' put in Sir Anthony.

'Quick of you for once, Kingston. The man must be given every latitude. We have to go through the motions at a leisurely pace, as if we had a completely open mind. When I say "we", I mean "I". The decision will be solely mine as to how the matter is put to the House of Commons.' The Lord Chancellor's tone changed from measured to malevolent. 'Now summon the bloody defendant, and let's get it over. It shouldn't take long, and then the Commons can chuck the bastard out.'

A moment later, Mr Justice Slingsby was ushered in. He carried a briefcase and was dressed in the customary black jacket and pin-striped trousers. The only discordant note was his garish tie, a brilliant abstract design worn as a defiant pennant.

'Ah, Mr Justice Slingsby.' Lord Trotter was doing his best to appear pleasant and finding it hard. 'Do sit down, please.' He indicated a Chippendale dining chair, which had been placed facing his desk.

'Do you wish to have somewhere to put your papers? I take it that is what you have in your case?'

'Not papers,' said Slingsby.

'Then what *do* you have in there, Slingsby? Nothing of a harmful nature, I trust.' Trot gave a wheezy chuckle.

'It could be. My wife prepared it.' This wasn't true – Janet had prepared his sandwiches – but Slingsby, who was feeling surprisingly cheerful, couldn't resist the crack.

Trot looked blank. 'Prepared what?'

'My lunch.'

'You have brought no documents?'

'They are up here.' Slingsby pointed to his head.

Trot decided it was time to get down to business. The man was plainly mad and the sooner this was over the better. 'Now. What do you wish to say? Take your time. I have an open mind.'

Slingsby looked him in the eye. 'Or is it an empty one, Lord Chancellor?'

The Lord Chancellor's face purpled slightly. 'Are you trying to make me hostile to you?'

'You are already, or I wouldn't be here. No-one has told me what charges I face. Even an unemployed layabout accused of having a bald tyre is entitled to that.'

Trot turned to his permanent secretary. 'Kingston?'

'The judge has had all the relevant documents,' murmured Sir Anthony.

'Good. Then you can present your case in any way you wish, judge.'

Slingsby smiled. 'It isn't my case. I didn't bring it. I want to hear the case against me. Who's the prosecutor. Is it Kingston?'

'There is no prosecutor, Slingsby.'

'Then I move the case be dismissed.' Slingsby picked up his briefcase as if to leave.

Trot's face was even more purple now. 'You must be serious about this. A great deal is at stake for you. Your problem is that you seem to find everything humorous. Entirely inappropriate for a High Court judge.'

'None of the documents complain about my sense of humour,' said Slingsby. 'Are you my prosecutor, then, Lord Chancellor? Or my judge? Or both? Are you trying to wear both wigs at once? Not very comfortable, surely.'

Trot rapped on the desk in frustration. 'You are being frivolous again, Slingsby. Is there or is there not anything further you wish to say?'

'A great deal. And I hope Mrs Chandelle-Sweet has a strong constitution. But you'd know about that, Lord Chancellor.'

'What are you implying?'

Slingsby looked from the Lord Chancellor to his secretary. 'That you've been having it off with her for years.'

There was a shriek from No-Knickers. Kingston put his head in his hands and surreptitiously tried to insert a finger in each ear.

'How dare you suggest such a thing?' said Trot furiously.

'Have you or haven't you? It's a simple question, Lord Chancellor,' Slingsby persisted.

'There is no reason why I should answer it.'

'Taking the Fifth Amendment? Very well, I'll put it to the lady herself. Has he been having you, or has he not, madam? And you'd better write down the answer, as well as say it.'

'You are confusing Mrs Chandelle-Sweet's roles,' snapped Trot.

'That's precisely what your lordship's been doing, isn't it?' said Slingsby nastily.

Trot realised that he was being manipulated and attempted to turn the tables on his enemy. 'I refuse to listen to any more of this, Slingsby. Even at this crucial moment, you are continuing your malicious campaign against me. I'm not certain if you realise the seriousness of your position – it was you who went to Ireland with a Page Three girl.'

'Yes, I did. In my own time. In whose time have you been having your private secretary? And on whose premises? I don't really care . . . '

'Then why raise it in this disgusting way?' interrupted Trot.

'I don't really care,' said Ray firmly, 'if you mount the lady outside in the street in the presence of twelve Horse Guards and their mounts. I do object to the way you tried to shut her husband's mouth by making him a judge. If that isn't corruption, I don't know what the word means.'

'Your suggestion is libellous.' Trot had now turned a deep shade of puce and Sir Anthony was beginning to worry about apoplexy.

'Oh, no, it isn't. It could be slanderous – but it happens to be true.'

'Prove it,' shouted Trot, beginning to lose control.

'I intend to. I intend to prove that you are a national disgrace, Lord Trotter, the worst holder ever of an office that is by its nature corrupt. All that power in one pair of hands is power gone mad.'

'Words, words, words, Slingsby,' mouthed the Lord Chancellor, eyes bulging. 'Not a shred of evidence.'

'Let me see Judge Chandelle-Sweet's file. You have it there, I take it?'

'It is you who are in the dock, Slingsby, not me. I'll thank you to remember that.'

'But I intend to put you in it, up to your neck, Lord Trotter. You and Kingston and this lady here – if she can be called a lady.'

The private secretary's face went white with rage, but she continued to struggle with her shorthand. The permanent secretary still had his head in his hands, and both head and hands now rested on the desk. Lord Trotter tried to pull himself together and counter-attack. He must remember that it was not himself on trial, but this upstart judge.

'Evidence. Where is the evidence, Mr Justice Raymond Slingsby?'

Ray was not as confident as he was trying to

appear. He knew he hadn't anything that would convince a court of law, though he felt sure that evidence against Trot existed. Could he somehow persuade the Lord Chancellor to let him probe more deeply?

Seeing him hesitate, Trot began to feel more confident. 'There, I told you so. Not got a shred of evidence, have you? That's because there's nothing in your absurd accusation. Nothing at all.' He looked at his subordinates. 'My staff know that as well as I do.'

Ray thought quickly. 'In that case, you won't mind me interviewing your staff to confirm it.'

'Eh, what?' Nonie and Kingston weren't going to condemn themselves, Trot decided, so he might as well let Slingsby make a fool of himself. 'If you must.'

'Then I'd like to call Elliott Standing. He is a member of your staff, is he not, Lord Chancellor?'

Nonie gasped and Sir Anthony groaned. Trot's mouth opened and shut but no sound came out.

'Elliott Standing,' repeated Slingsby. 'You did offer to let me interview your staff, as I see Mrs Chandelle-Sweet has kindly noted down.'

Trot cursed inwardly. The transcript could not be altered – he had blundered into a trap. Sir Anthony looked at him questioningly and he made an exasperated motion with his hand. The permanent secretary sprang from the room like a startled hare and returned almost immediately with Standing, who appeared both puzzled and alarmed.

'Mr Justice Slingsby has some questions to put

to you, Standing,' Trot ground out through gritted teeth. 'You are not obliged to answer any that may incriminate you.' He glared at the man in a threatening way.

'Incriminate me?' Standing looked terrified. 'What am I supposed to have done?'

'Don't upset yourself, Standing.' Slingsby realised this was going to be the most important cross-examination he had ever conducted. 'I believe you were recently in the Lord Chancellor's flat upstairs, delivering something urgent. And you witnessed something between the Lord Chancellor and Mrs Chandelle-Sweet.'

'Did I?'

'You were there. *I'm* asking *you*. Something of an affectionate nature.'

'Don't lead the witness.' Lord Trotter was becoming technical and also apprehensive.

'What did you see, Standing?'

Standing gazed hopelessly round the room as if looking for inspiration.

'Do you recall how Lord Trotter and Mrs Chandelle-Sweet were standing?' Ray pressed him.

'Together,' said Standing, thinking that this sounded harmless enough.

'Please demonstrate.'

Here the Lord Chancellor intervened to point out that as the witness was only one person, it might be difficult for him to demonstrate what two people were doing – not that they were doing anything at all, he added quickly. The judge was not to be deterred. He asked if Mrs Chandelle-

283

Sweet could stand next to the witness, apologising for interrupting her note-taking. The secretary indicated a small tape-recorder in front of her, 'as back-up'.

She moved over beside Standing, who, after a brief hesitation, held out a tentative hand towards her midriff.

Ray's eyes brightened. 'What was the Lord Chancellor doing with his hand?' he asked Standing.

'Well – touching her hand, I think.'

'As if doing what?'

Standing glanced at the Lord Chancellor. 'Shaking hands, I suppose.'

'With his private secretary, who had already been in his flat for at least three-quarters of an hour that morning?' said Ray. 'I find that hard to believe.'

But now that Standing had found his story, he was sticking to it, and when Ray suggested that he might have been got at, the Lord Chancellor objected violently to this entirely improper suggestion, made wholly without foundation.

One last effort by Ray. 'Was his Lordship doing or trying to do towards Mrs Chandelle-Sweet, anything additional to shaking hands?'

'Not that I saw.' Standing was not to be moved.

'Then you'd better get back to your pen-pushing,' said Ray in exasperation,

'Is that your case, Slingsby?' Lord Trotter asked, in a tone of quiet triumph.

'No.' Ray was not finished yet. 'I demand to see the Chandelle-Sweet file.'

'Request refused. Private and confidential. Official Secrets Act.'

'It's been repealed.'

'There's another one. I rely on that.'

'Then I insist on an adjournment, so I can apply to the High Court for an order that you produce it.'

'What authority have you for doing that, Slingsby?'

'I shall explain that in court.' Mr Justice Slingsby was bluffing; he did not know of any statute or case in his favour. He felt as if he was back at the Bar. 'Does your Lordship allow me to see the file, or do I go immediately to the High Court?'

'They won't decide in your favour.'

'I realise you appointed most of them. And they look to you for promotion,' said Ray.

The confounded persistence of the man was beginning to wear Trot down. He wasn't used to being contradicted or questioned, and the whole situation was beginning to confuse him. The bullying tactics that had always served him so well in the past seemed to be having no effect, but he tried once more. 'Slingsby, are you accusing your fellow High Court judges of bias?' he roared, pounding his desk with his fist.

'Yes,' said Ray quietly. 'Now may I see the file, or may I not?'

'No. I forbid it. You are determined to destroy the good name of the judiciary, and my good name, and I won't let you do it.'

'Do you possess a good name?' The expression on Trot's face made Ray wonder if even he had gone too far this time. Scowling frightfully, the Lord Chancellor heaved his huge bulk up from the desk. I'll kill the bastard, thought Trot, but as he started to move towards Ray he felt a sharp twinge of pain in his chest. All at once he remembered his doctor's warnings about his high blood pressure. Collapsing like a pricked balloon he slumped back in his chair.

The pain ebbed away, but Trot was so overcome by anger, frustration and fear that he could hardly speak. He heard Slingsby saying that he had further questions for Mrs Chandelle-Sweet, and he could only sit and glower as the judge's cross-examination began.

'Madam, many employers make advances to their female employees, do they not?'

'Do they?' said Anona innocently. She had realised at once that something was wrong with Trot, but after the way he'd behaved recently she thought it served him right. *When* she was good and ready she might offer to get him a glass of water or something, but first she would answer the judge's questions.

'Have you not read about it in the press? You know the sort of thing. "He pestered me and kept putting his arm round me and touching me."'

'I – I'm not sure.' I wouldn't mind Slingsby pestering me, thought Anona.

'The Lord Chancellor may dress up as Widow Twanky in Cinderella for his job downstairs, but underneath he's a man, like any other man. He isn't gay, is he?'

Anona hid a smile. 'Oh no, not gay, I'm sure he's not.'

'How do you know?'

'Well I just would, wouldn't I? People talk – other civil servants.'

'What *do* they say about your employer's sexual activities?'

'I don't know.' Anona looked down demurely.

'But if they talk, they must use words. What words?'

'You are bullying my secretary,' Trotter croaked. He was feeling slightly better now.

'Some may think *you* bullied this lady, Lord Chancellor. Did he, madam? *Did* he?'

'Most bosses do, at times,' murmured Anona.

'Did you have rows?'

Anona glanced at Trot, and made up her mind. 'We had one today, as a matter of fact.'

'What about?'

'Privilege, that's privileged,' the Lord Chancellor muttered.

'So it *did* happen.' Ray let this sink in, then there was a brief pause before he changed tack. 'Mrs Chandelle-Sweet, were you surprised when your boss turned your husband into a judge?'

'Well, no, actually I wasn't.'

'Would you care to look at the file on your husband?'

'I forbid it,' gasped the Lord Chancellor, but no one took any notice of him.

'Have you ever looked in it, madam?'

'In the course of my work,' Anona admitted.

'Then look at it again, please, to refresh your memory. I am not asking to see it myself.'

In the absence of any direction to the contrary from the Lord Chancellor, Sir Anthony Kingston handed the file to Anona.

'Find me one favourable remark about your husband in that file, if you can.'

'There isn't one,' said Anona in a firm voice. 'I know that already.'

Ray smiled encouragingly. 'Can you tell me of any instance you know of where a judge has been appointed, although everybody whose opinion has been asked has been against him? You must have seen dozens of files.'

'I have – but I've never seen another like Alwyne's.'

'So if your husband is incompetent, there must be some other reason for making him a judge. Do you agree?'

There was a pause. Anona knew how she was going to answer, but she wanted to prolong the agony for Trot.

'Come along, madam,' urged Ray, sensing that she was close to giving him what he wanted. 'I must have an answer. Was the reason for your husband's appointment that you and Lord Trotter were having an affair and your husband found out? It was to keep him quiet, buy his silence, wasn't it, madam?'

Another short silence, broken only by the sound of Trot's heavy breathing. Then Anona said, quietly. 'Yes, it's true. That's exactly what did happen. Lord Trotter's been having sex with me for over two years.'

'And there's the evidence,' said Raymond Slingsby in triumph, as he grabbed the tape-recorder that stood in front of her.

'Put that down. It's government property. Official Secrets Act.' The Lord Chancellor struggled to rise from his chair, then fell back again, clutching his chest.

'At the moment, it's mine.' Ray dropped the tape recorder into his briefcase. 'Goodbye, Lord Chancellor, I think our interview has served its purpose.'

He hurried from the room, leaving Anona and Sir Anthony staring after him in astonishment. They did not move for some moments, until roused by a feeble cry from their employer, 'For God's sake, somebody, call a doctor. I think I'm having a bloody heart attack.'

12

Rᴀʏ ʀᴇᴛᴜʀɴᴇᴅ to the flat brimming with confidence.

'I've got him,' he said to Janet. 'It's all on here.' He tossed the tape towards her.

'Darling, you are clever.' Janet threw her arms round him and kissed him passionately. Then they sat down to listen to the tape, eager to hear the vital evidence.

The tape-recorder whirred, hissed and crackled, but no words came out. Janet picked it up and fiddled with it. Then she rewound the tape and tried again. It was no good. The tape was blank. Anona Chandelle-Sweet's admissions had never been recorded.

Ray and Janet looked at each other in despair. Both knew only too well what this meant. Ray still had no firm evidence against Trotter. The Lord Chancellor would certainly deny his private secretary's allegations, and Kingston would be sure to support him.

'I'll try Mrs Chandelle-Sweet,' said Janet, trying

to salvage something from the wreck. 'If she's prepared to repeat in public what she said this morning, we could still be all right.'

She rang the Lord Chancellor's office. Mrs Chandelle-Sweet came to the phone. She was pleasant enough, although she sounded a little distracted, but she was clearly in no mood to give anything more away. She told Janet that if she talked to the media, it would jeopardise her career as a civil servant, and that anyway she certainly did not recall admitting that her employer had had sex with her.

While she blocked Janet's questions, Anona was thinking fast. The only possible reason that she could imagine for the call was that Janet had been talking to Ray Slingsby. But after all Slingsby should now have all the information he needed on the tape that he had taken. If Janet now wanted Slingsby's story confirmed, that must mean the tape was a blank. She had probably pressed the wrong button in her agitation – she never had been very good with mechanical objects.

Anona smiled to herself as she brought the conversation to a close, considering what she would do with this information. 'No, I'm sorry, I'm afraid I can't comment on any of your suggestions. You must understand, I have to think of my own future now.'

Janet was so annoyed that she did not take very much notice of this last bit. She assumed it meant that Trotter was sacking Anona, and that she would have to look for another job. 'Serve her right, snotty cow,' she fumed, but insulting Anona Chandelle-Sweet didn't make the picture look any brighter.

Trot was bound to win now, Ray said gloomily. He had evidence from Dublin that Ray could not deny, and the story of a sex orgy in a land forbidden to an English High Court judge was not going to lie down and go away. On the other hand, Ray could not prove that the appointment of Judge Sweet was corrupt. The Lord Chancellor decided who should be judges and mistakes were bound to happen occasionally. Mr Justice Slingsby had made baseless allegations of adultery and corruption against a senior government minister, and the Commons were certain to act on that in support of 'the other place'.

Ray kissed Janet goodbye, and they clung together for a moment, trying to give each other some comfort. Then he left for Barfield. He had to see Helen and prepare himself for his dismissal by Her Majesty. His instinct was to fight on, but without ammunition it was hopeless. He was not going to continue in hiding, however, and he would face the media barrage, trying to smile even as he sank under the waves.

Ray did not go to the Judges' Lodgings but to his own house in Barfield. As he got out of the taxi, he ran over in his mind the little speech he had prepared on the train journey up from London. It was nothing less than an abject apology, and a promise that if Helen would stand by him now he would never stray in future. He had decided, painfully, in the course of the past few hours that although he was sure he cared deeply for Janet, he owed it to Helen to try and save their marriage. He had behaved appallingly, but now he would try and do the decent thing – he had sighted freedom, but his puritan conscience had got the better of him. The trap was closed once more.

He approached the house, and was surprised to see that there were full milk-bottles on the doorstep. A newspaper was stuck in the letter-box, and when he unlocked the door and opened it, the morning's post was on the mat. Ray called, but there was no reply. The house was empty.

Beginning to guess what had happened, he went into the kitchen. There on the table was a letter in Helen's writing, addressed to him. As Ray read it, he laughed at himself for being such a fool. Helen had gone to stay with her mother and would not be coming back. Ray had made their life together impossible, she wrote, and she had decided on a permanent separation. Ray sat down at the kitchen table and stared into nothingness. This was the lowest point in his life. He wondered if he could possibly sink any lower. There was nothing left except disaster and disgrace.

He rang the Lodgings and spoke to the butler. A new judge had already been sent from London to replace him. All avenues were blocked. Life was bleak beyond endurance. Ray had tried to get the system improved but it had all come unstuck. He would be plastered across the tabloids as a disgraced judge – an ex-judge. A man nobody would want to know. Even Janet, he thought, would not want him now. Taking the only avenue he could see open, Mr Justice Raymond Slingsby, as he still was, took out a bottle of Jameson's whiskey he had brought from Ireland and began to empty it. There was a little left in the bottle when he slumped into a stupor and fell asleep, still in the kitchen chair.

Soon after seven o'clock the following morning, Page Three girl Sarah Garrowby sat in her Clapham bed-sitter feeling sorry for herself. The Irish adventure had been a disaster. She had never been arrested before and hoped it would never happen again. It did not go with her image. She had expected publicity that would portray her as the innocent victim she was, and had prepared herself for the press at the airport but – nothing had happened. Her agent was trying to sell her story, but the papers didn't want to know. They were full of news about Terry Whitstable, Minister for Recreation, who had taken the widest interpretation of the word 'recreation' in playing with several Page Three girls at once.

That was overdoing it a bit, Sarah thought, and what was more it made her exploits with the judge look extremely tame. She still had not been offered any more modelling jobs, dressed or undressed, and she wondered if her boobs were going off. Plastic surgery might be the answer, but she didn't fancy some knife-happy surgeon getting hold of her. As for becoming an actress, her agent had told her during their last conversation that even girls who had been to RADA were out of work, so she didn't see much hope of that.

The newspapers had just arrived and out of

professional interest, Sarah was glancing at Page Three in the *Sun*, when she noticed a small item at the foot of a column on the opposite page. An unidentified middle-aged man had been found dead in an old Volvo estate-car. A pipe led from the exhaust to the interior, and the police would issue a statement about his identity later that day. 'Who can that be?' Sarah wondered. Some poor sod who'd had enough of life. Well she hadn't. Life wasn't as bad as that. There were things to do and enjoy, especially men. There were still plenty of those around. Most of them wanted one thing, and that was something she still had, even if they didn't always get it straight away – she had her rules. It was a great game though, sex, the best God ever invented.

Up in Barfield, Ray was still fast asleep, draped over the kitchen table. He stirred uncomfortably as the sound of a telephone drilled into his brain, then, as the ringing persisted, staggered to his feet to answer it. On the other end of the line was Janet, sounding wildly excited. She had just heard on the news that Lord Chancellor Trotter had resigned.

In a letter that had been released to the media, the Lord Chancellor had written to the Prime Minister stating that owing to his poor health he had decided to hand over his office, he hoped to a younger man who would be better equipped to carry the heavy burden involved. The letter went on to say that Trotter had also decided to withdraw all proceedings against Mr Justice Slingsby, in order to give him the benefit of the doubt and to show that, whatever mistakes he,

Trotter, may have made, he was at bottom an indulgent man. Both Houses of Parliament were being informed and the judge's reputation and record remained unblemished.

Ray was stunned. He couldn't believe what he was hearing. The Lord Chancellor resign? It was the one solution to his problems of which he had never even dared to dream. As Janet continued to gabble in his ear, he tried to gather his scattered thoughts.

'Ray, Ray, are you still there? Isn't it wonderful news?' Janet's voice sounded anxious and he realised he still hadn't responded.

'Yes, of course, it's unbelievable. I don't understand it at all, though.'

Janet laughed. 'You must have done something to him at that interview. How did he look when you left him?'

Ray thought back. 'Not too good, certainly, but I can't believe I upset him that much. No, it's a complete mystery to me.'

'Never mind,' said Janet. 'Just be grateful it's happened.'

With growing relief and delight, Ray began to take in the implications of what she had told him. But I'll still make that speech at Chesterfield, even though there's no need to attack Trotter, was his first thought. Then he thought again. It would cause so much trouble, and he wondered if he could stand being the centre of another uproar just yet. Perhaps there should be a time for quiet reflection before his next assault on the system.

He was free now, he realised. Free to do

whatever he wanted. 'I think I'd like a holiday,' he said. If ever a man deserved a proper break, he did, and he knew who he would like to join him.

Janet spared him the trouble of asking. This was no time for hanging back, Janet decided. She wanted this man, and she knew what would tempt him most. 'Let me take you to the Med, Ray. We'll hire a boat and go island-hopping.'

Raymond Slingsby sighed happily. In his mind, he was already packing brushes, paints, palette, and easel. He would also need a bathing-costume – but only when there were other people around.

Anona Chandelle-Sweet sat on her husband's bed in his private room at St Felix's, eating the grapes she had brought him. It was her first visit since Alwyne had been taken there, and he was very pleased to see her, although a little confused as to what had been going on in her absence.

'So you say the Lord Chancellor's resigning? And is the poor man really ill?'

'Oh, no,' said Anona, spitting out a grape pip, 'that was just a touch of indigestion. He's fine. It gave him a bit of a fright, that's all.'

Alwyne looked puzzled. 'In that case, I don't quite see why he's resigning.'

'It made him think about the future.' Anona smiled. 'He's not getting any younger, you know.' She did not tell her husband that Trotter still believed that her admissions about their affair were on the tape that Slingsby had taken. She was certainly not going to let the disgusting old fool of a lord chancellor know that the tape was a blank –

let him go, and good riddance to him, she thought.

'Oh, I see.' Alwyne snuggled back against his pillows, content with her explanation. 'And I can go on being a judge.'

'I expect so,' said Anona, 'as long as you don't do anything silly.' She smiled again. 'And I'm going to be secretary to the new Lord Chancellor.'

Warner now offers an exciting range of quality titles by both established and new authors. All of the books in this series are available from:
Little, Brown and Company (UK),
P.O. Box 11,
Falmouth,
Cornwall TR10 9EN.

Alternatively you may fax your order to the above address. Fax No. 0326 376423.

Payments can be made as follows: Cheque, postal order (payable to Little, Brown and Company) or by credit cards, Visa/Access. Do not send cash or currency. UK customers: and B.F.P.O.: please send a cheque or postal order (no currency) and allow £1.00 for postage and packing for the first book, plus 50p for the second book, plus 30p for each additional book up to a maximum charge of £3.00 (7 books plus).

Overseas customers including Ireland, please allow £2.00 for postage and packing for the first book, plus £1.00 for the second book, plus 50p for each additional book.

NAME (Block Letters) ....

ADDRESS...

....

☐ I enclose my remittance for _____

☐ I wish to pay by Access/Visa Card

Number ☐☐☐☐☐☐☐☐☐☐☐☐☐☐☐☐☐☐

Card Expiry Date ☐☐☐☐